Learn to Cook
Healthy Asian
Vegetarian Dishes

Your guide to the exciting world of Asian vegetarian cooking.
Contains over 75 flavorful recipes that can
be prepared at home in minutes.

PERIPLUS

Contents

MAIL ORDER SOURCES

Finding the ingredients for Asian home cooking has become very simple. Most supermarkets carry staples such as soy sauce, fresh ginger, and fresh lemongrass. Almost every large metropolitan area has Asian markets serving the local population—just check your local business directory. With the Internet, exotic Asian ingredients and cooking utensils can be easily found online. The following list is a good starting point of online merchants offering a wide variety of goods and services.

http://www.asiafoods.com
http://www.geocities.com/MadisonAvenue/8074/VarorE.html
http://dmoz.org/Shopping/Food/Ethnic_and_Regional/Asian/
http://templeofthai.com/
http://www.orientalpantry.com/
http://www.zestyfoods.com/
http://www.thaigrocer.com/Merchant/index.htm
http://asianwok.com/
http://pilipinomart.com/
http://www.indiangrocerynet.com/
http://www.orientalfoodexpress.com/

Vegetarian cooking has long been an integral part of Asia's culinary landscape, with many groups of peoples in India, China, Thailand, Vietnam, Korea and other parts of Asia foregoing meat primarily due to religious reasons. This book presents a mouthwatering selection of vegetarian recipes drawn from many different regions of Asia — which are not only extremely nutritious but also simple to prepare and fabulously tasty!

Asian vegetarian cooking differs greatly from the vegetarian fare normally found in Western countries. Extensive use is made of fresh tropical spices, fragrant herbs, exotic vegetables and fruits. Foremost among these are the spicy chili pepper used to impart a pungent bite to many Asian dishes. Sesame oil, toasted sesame seeds or sesame paste, garlic, ginger, galangal, black pepper, fermented black beans and soy sauce are essential ingredients in any Asian larder. And herbs like Asian basil, curry leaves, coriander leaves (cilantro) and mint add zest to sauces and stir-fries, or a bright splash of color when used as a garnish.

Two mainstays of the vegetarian diet in Asia are protein-rich tofu (bean curd) and dried or fresh *shiitake* or Chinese black mushrooms. Tofu comes in a wide variety of forms and flavors, and is prepared in an incredible number of different ways — eaten plain with soy sauce and pickled turnips, deep-fried with garlic and a bit of salt, "crinkle-fried" with vegetables, stir-fried with seasonings — the list goes on and on. *Shiitake* mushrooms have a similar versatility, as well as an exceptionally high nutritional content, and Chinese or Japanese vegetarian meals would be unthinkable without them.

The sheer variety of vegetables found in Asia is incredible, and over many centuries, Asians have developed endless ways of preparing them — each more delicious than the last! All the usual Western vegetables such as cabbage, spinach, potatoes, tomatoes, carrots, etc., are widely eaten, but so are many less common ones like lotus root, mung bean sprouts, bok choy, choy sum, water convolvulus, and so forth. One of the most exciting things about Asian cooking is exploring the new tastes and textures these unusual vegetables provide. And so many of them are now available in health food stores or Asian food shops!

The staples of an Asian vegetarian meal are rice or noodles combined with some sort of sauce. Indian vegetable curries generally feature a range of protein-rich legumes and pulses, cooked in half a dozen or more flavorful spices — often with coconut milk or tamarind added. Rice is of course eaten plain with other side dishes and condiments, or prepared in various ways with spices and herbs.

While millions of Asians are vegetarians for religious reasons, there are a growing number who practise it due to health concerns or as a lifestyle choice. As a result, nowhere else in the world is vegetarianism so widespread, and nowhere else can you find such a variety of delicious vegetarian recipes!

Ingredients Glossary

Agar-agar is a type of gelatin derived from seaweed. It is used in setting puddings and other desserts.

Asian eggplants are long and slender, smaller and slightly sweeter than the commonplace Western variety. Available in purple or green.

Black bean paste is made from fermented soy beans and salt. It has a strong, salty flavor.

Black moss fungus, also known as "angel hair", is a fine, fiber-like fungus that is added to Chinese soups or used as a garnish in some Chinese dishes. It should be soaked in warm water until it becomes soft.

Bok choy is a crunchy, green leafy vegetable that will keep for about one week in a refrigerator, although it tastes best when used fresh. It may be substituted by mustard greens or cabbage.

Cardamom is the pod of a tree that is used to flavor many Indian dishes. Both green and black cardamoms are available. Green cardamoms are normally used for flavoring desserts and tea. Black cardamoms are often used in meat and vegetable curries and pickles. Cardamom is available in Indian and health food stores and is one of the ingredients used in the spice mixture, *garam masala*.

Cayenne pepper is a pungent red powder made from ground chili peppers, also known as ground red pepper. Substitute with dried red chili flakes or chili paste.

Chili paste is a bottled sauce made from whole ground chili peppers sold in many grocery stores. To the chilies are generally added a combination of salt, sugar, garlic and sometimes soy beans or ginger. Chili paste comes in many flavors ranging from sweet to spicy.

Chinese celery has slender stems and pungent leaves. It is smaller than Western celery and is used as an herb and added to soups, rice dishes and stir-fries. Substitute with Western celery leaves.

Choy sum is used in Chinese stir-fry dishes and soups. It is similar to bok choy, but has more tender and delicious stems and flower buds. It may be substituted with mustard greens or bok choy.

Coconut milk is made by blending the freshly grated flesh of a mature coconut with about 1 cup (250 ml) water, and then squeezing the liquid out of it. Coconut milk is very rich and high in cholesterol. Substitute with normal milk. Canned coconut milk is now widely available in most supermarkets.

Coriander leaves, also known as cilantro, are widely used as a flavoring and garnish. Fresh coriander leaves have a strong taste and aroma and can be refrigerated in a plastic bag for about one week. Parsley is a suitable substitute. **Coriander seeds** are used as a spice in Asian curries.

Curry leaves are used in Indian dishes in much the same way as basil or oregano are used in Italian cooking — to add aroma and flavor to the sauce. Fresh curry leaves should be used within a few days of purchase. Dried curry leaves keep well if they are stored in a dry place.

Daikon is a large, white radish or carrot used in Chinese and Japanese cooking. It can be eaten raw or cooked and is often pickled. Used mainly in soups and stir-fries, it is available in Asian grocery stores and many supermarkets now.

Fenugreek seeds are used in many Indian curries. These yellowish brown seeds have little aroma until dry-roasted and ground. **Fenugreek leaves** are used as an herb in Indian cooking. Both are available in Indian grocery stores and health food stores.

Five-spice powder is a Chinese ground spice combination of star anise, Sichuan peppercorns, fennel, cloves and cinnamon. It is used in meat marinades and soup stocks. This mixture is very strong, and should be used in small amounts.

Galangal is a member of the ginger family. It is pinkish or creamy orange-white and has a sharp and pungent taste. It is commonly used in Thai, Malaysian and Indonesian cuisines, and is sold fresh in Asian markets; substitute with ginger.

Garam masala is an Indian blend of strong aromatic spices used to add flavor and fragrance to curries. Powdered *garam masala* can be bought from Indian or South Asian grocery stores. Store in a jar in the freezer.

Ghee is the rich, delicious clarified butter oil used as the main oil in Indian cooking. It is made from cow or water buffalo milk by removing the milk solids from the oil. It keeps well at room temperature. Substitute with vegetable oil or butter.

Hoisin sauce is a sweet sauce made of soy beans and is used as a dipping sauce and flavoring. Refrigerate after opening.

Jicama is a crunchy, mild tuber with a crisp white interior and beige skin, which peels off easily. Excellent eaten raw with a spicy dip, it is also known as a yam bean and can be used as a substitute for lotus root.

Kaffir lime leaves are the fragrant leaves of the kaffir lime plant. The leaves are used whole in soups and curries, or shredded finely and added to salads.

Konbu refers to dried sea kelp usually sold in flat black sheets with white powder on the surface which must be removed before cooking.

Lentils are protein- and fiber-rich legumes often referred to in Asia by their Indian name, *dal*. Five kinds of lentils are used in this book. **Split chickpeas** or garbanzos (*channa dal*) resemble yellow split peas, which may be used as a substitute. **Split mung beans** (*mung dal*) are the split, husked version of the same bean used to make bean sprouts — pale yellow, slightly elongated and popular in northern Indian cooking. **Split yellow lentils** (*tur dal* or *tuvar dal*) are pale yellow in color and smaller than chickpeas. **Black lentils** (*urad dal*) are sold either with their black skin on or husked, when they become creamy white in color. **Split red lentils** (*masoor dal*) are light orange when raw and turn yellow when cooked. **Lotus root** is the thick root of the aquatic lotus plant and is available fresh in many Chinese grocery stores. It is either covered in mud or cleaned and scaled and wrapped in plastic. A good substitute is jicama (yam bean) or cauliflower.

Lotus seeds can be seen at the tops of lotus pods as the pods ripen. They have a nutty flavor and are used in soups and stews. In some Asian countries, they are used to make desserts.

Mushrooms are prized in Asian cooking for the flavor and texture they add to dishes. *Shiitake* or Chinese black mushrooms are generally large and meaty, and are used in soups, stir-fries and side dishes, or as a meat substitute. Substitute with porcini mushrooms. Fresh *shiitake* are increasingly available in supermarkets. Fresh, delicately sheathed **straw mushrooms** are excellent in soups and vegetable dishes. **Button mushrooms** and large, bland **oyster mushrooms** are good for stir-frying. *Enokitaki* **(golden mushrooms)** are clusters of slender, cream-colored stalks with tiny caps, and are available fresh and tinned. The tough ends of the *enokitaki* should be discarded before use.

Noodles are widely used in Asian cooking. They generally come in different widths ranging from fine vermicelli-like noodles to broad, flat noodles. **Wheat noodles** are made with wheat flour, water, and sometimes eggs. **Rice noodles** are made with rice flour. **Mung bean** or **glass noodles** are thin, transparent noodles made from mung beans and they readily absorb other flavors in a dish. Substitute with rice vermicelli or angel hair pasta. Dried Asian noodles can be found in most supermarkets. Fresh Asian noodles are more easily found in Asian grocery stores or markets.

Palm sugar is made from the refined sap of the sugar palm. Available in Asian grocery stores, it is usually sold in small disks that are $1/2$-in (1-cm) thick and 3-in ($7^1/_2$-cm) wide, or are sometimes sold in larger cellophane-wrapped blocks. Palm sugar may be substituted with dark brown sugar or maple syrup.

Pickled turnips are traditionally colored by adding sliced raw beetroot to the pickling jar. The cherry-colored juices penetrate the white turnips, giving them a pinkish to reddish color depending on the amount of beetroot.

Plantains look like huge bananas, but are not as sweet and much firmer. They are available in many Hispanic markets and may be substituted with pumpkin.

Pumpkins are used in sweet dishes such as desserts and in soups. They are eaten when fully ripe and their flesh is high in fiber and has an earthy flavor.

Red dates are about the size of a round olive, and taste sour when raw but are sweet when matured and dried.

Rice wine or *sake* adds a sweet, subtle flavor to dishes. It is used in Chinese cooking as a tenderizer, to blend flavors and enhance taste. It is widely available in Asian grocery stores and the specialty food section of some supermarkets. Dry sherry is a good substitute.

Sesame paste is made from ground, roasted sesame seeds. The paste can be quite hard and should be mixed with a little sesame oil or water to make it into a smooth paste. Sesame paste should not be confused with the sweet sesame paste made from black sesame seeds that is used in some cakes and desserts. Substitute with Middle Eastern tahini mixed with sesame oil to give it a more pronounced flavor.

Sichuan pepper, also known as flower pepper or fagara, has a sharp pungence that tingles and slightly numbs the lips and tongue, an effect known in Chinese as *ma la* ("numb hot"). To make Sichuan Pepper-salt Powder, dry-toast Sichuan peppercorns with salt (2 tablespoons Sichuan peppercorns to $1/2$ teaspoon salt), grind to a fine powder and sprinkle over cooked dishes as garnish.

Soy beans are an abundant source of high quality vegetable protein and oil, and contain virtually no cholesterol. They are a rich source of vitamin B, minerals and fiber.

Soy sauce is fermented from soya beans and salt, and is commonly used in marinades, sauces and dips. Two different types are widely used in Asian cooking. **Thick soy sauce** is often added to give a dark coloring and strong, smoky flavor to a dish. **Light soy sauce** is thinner, lighter in color and saltier than black soy sauce. Low salt varieties are also available. Poor-quality soy sauce can ruin the taste of even the best food, so it's well worth spending a bit more for higher-grade soy sauce.

Star anise is a dark brown, strongly-flavored spice that resembles an eight-pointed star. Its aroma is similar to anise or cinnamon. Store in a tightly-sealed jar in a cool, dry place.

Tamarind pulp comes from the pods of the tamarind tree. It is usually sold in cellophane-wrapped squares or jars with the seeds removed and the flesh compressed. The pulp is the key ingredient in **tamarind juice**, a sour liquid that adds intense flavor to many Asian dishes. To make tamarind juice, soak 3 tablespoons of tamarind pulp in $1^1/2$ cups (375 ml) warm water for 20 minutes. Squeeze the pulp, stir the mixture well, then strain the mixture and discard the solids.

Tofu (bean curd) is available firm or soft. **Firm tofu** stays in shape when cut or cooked and has a stronger, slightly sour taste. **Soft tofu** is slippery and tends to crumble easily but has a more silky texture and refined flavor. **Tofu skin** is the thin rich layer of soy protein that forms on the surface of soy bean milk while it is being boiled to make tofu. The dried variety, or **tofu sheet**, is available in most Asian grocery stores. It has the same nutritional benefits and is easier to work with in the kitchen, although it is less tasty than tofu skin. Tofu sheet is commonly used in stir-fries and vegetarian cooking as a meat substitute.

Vegetarian mushroom oyster sauce is a soy-based sauce that is the vegetarian substitute for regular oyster sauce.

Water convolvulus is also known as water spinach and by its Malay name *kangkung*. This aquatic plant is rich in protein and minerals such as iron.

White fungus is also known as dried white wood ears. It is a crinkly golden dried fungus that becomes transparent after soaking. It adds a crunchy texture to dishes and is often used in Chinese soups and desserts.

Wood ear fungus is a type of mushroom that grows on trees and are also known as tree ear mushrooms. These mild-flavored mushrooms are sold dried in Asian grocery stores and are reconstituted by soaking in water.

Chinese Bean Sprout Salad with Garlic Dressing

Most Chinese salads are made with vegetables that have been lightly blanched, and the range of ingredients used for salads in Chinese cuisine is much broader than those in the West. The actual word for "salad" courses in Chinese is *leng pan*, which simply means "cold dish." This could refer to platters of cold cuts, tofu, beans, and anything else served cold.

$1/_4$ lb (125 g) fresh
  soy bean sprouts, rinsed
$1/_4$ lb (125 g) fresh mung
  bean sprouts, rinsed
1 teaspoon salt
2 fresh scallions, finely
  chopped (optional)

Sauce
2 to 3 cloves garlic, finely
  minced
2 tablespoons soy sauce
1 tablespoon sesame oil
1 teaspoon sugar
$1/_2$ teaspoon salt
$1/_2$ teaspoon freshly
  ground black pepper
1 teaspoon vinegar

1 Mix together all the sauce ingredients and set aside.
2 Bring a large pot of water to a rolling boil and add 1 teaspoon salt.
3 Add the soy bean sprouts to the boiling water and blanch for about 2 minutes. Remove with slotted spoon and let drain in a colander.
4 Add the mung bean sprouts to the boiling water and blanch for about 20 seconds. Drain and set aside.
5 Mix the two kinds of sprouts together in a bowl, then add the sauce and toss well. Garnish with chopped scallions, if desired.

Serves 4
Preparation time: 10 mins
Cooking time: 5 mins

Vegetarian Appetizer Plate

Three 8-in (20-cm) strips dried *konbu*, soaked in water for 40 minutes, rinsed and drained
2 pieces dried tofu
1 medium carrot, peeled and sliced
8 large dried *shiitake* mushrooms, rinsed and soaked in hot water for 15 minutes
1 medium *daikon*, peeled and cubed
$1/4$ cup wood ear fungus, rinsed, soaked and drained, stems removed
1 in ($2^1/2$ cm) fresh ginger, grated
1 fresh chili, halved
1 medium broccoli, cut into florets
$1/2$ head iceberg lettuce, separated into leaves

Stock
4 cups (1 liter) water
$1/2$ tablespoon five-spice powder
1 teaspoon salt
2 teaspoons sugar
2 tablespoons rice wine
$1/3$ cup (85 ml) soy sauce

Dips
Hot Chinese or English mustard
Soy Sauce
Toasted sesame seeds
Sweet Thai chili sauce

1 To prepare the seaweed bundles, roll up each piece of soaked *konbu* to form a roll, then pierce it with a toothpick to secure and set aside.

2 To prepare the stock, bring 4 cups water to the boil in a large pot. Add the remaining seasonings and return to the boil.

3 Add tofu and all vegetables, except the broccoli and lettuce leaves. When it returns to the boil, cover and reduce heat to low, and cook for 20 to 30 minutes. Stir gently once or twice to prevent sticking. After 20 minutes, add the broccoli. If vegetables become too dry, add $1/2$ cup (125 ml) water.

4 Meanwhile, line a serving dish with the lettuce leaves.

5 When tender, drain vegetables in a colander, reserving the stock. Discard ginger and chili.

6 When cool enough to handle, cut the tofu squares and mushrooms into bite-sized pieces; remove toothpicks from seaweed rolls and cut each roll into thin slices. Arrange all cut ingredients on platter.

7 Warm the stock in a small saucepan and drizzle 2 tablespoons of the stock evenly onto the cut ingredients and serve.

8 Serve with hot Chinese or English mustard, wasabi, soy sauce, toasted sesame seeds or sweet Thai chili sauce.

Serves 4
Preparation time: 20 mins + 40 mins soaking time
Cooking time: 1 hour 20 mins

Tofu Skin Rolls with Sesame Ginger Sauce

2 cups (200 g) fresh
  mung bean sprouts,
  blanched
1/2 cup (50 g) *enokitaki*
  mushrooms, separated,
  cleaned, and blanched
2 medium carrots,
  peeled, shredded,
  and blanched
1 cup (110 g) sugar
  snap or snow peas,
  sliced lengthways and
  blanched
4 sheets dried tofu skin
1 tablespoon all-purpose
  flour
2 tablespoons oil

Sauce
2 tablespoons sesame
  paste or tahini, blended
  with 5 teaspoons water
1/2 teaspoon thick soy
  sauce
1/2 teaspoon salt
3 1/2 teaspoons sugar
4 teaspoons vinegar
1 teaspoon sesame oil
2 cloves garlic, minced
1 scallion, thinly sliced
2 slices fresh ginger,
  minced
1 fresh red chili, seeded
  and minced

1 Bring a large pot of lightly salted water to the boil and add the bean sprouts , mushrooms, carrots, and sugar snaps. Stir a few times, leave in water about 30 seconds, then remove to a colander, rinse in cool water, drain, and set aside.

2 Cut each sheet tofu skin in half. Place one half atop the other. Repeat, ending up with 4 layered rectangles about 8 x 10 in (20 x 25 cm).

3 Place the vegetables in a mixing bowl, and sprinkle evenly with the flour and mix. Divide the vegetables evenly into 4 portions, and place them neatly at the edge of each of the 4 rectangles. Roll the skins over the vegetables to form tubes. To prevent tofu skin from opening up while frying, seal the skin with paste made from flour and water.

4 Heat the oil in a large skillet over high heat and when oil is hot but not smoking, gently place the tofu skin rolls in the pan and fry about 2 minutes, then turn and fry the other side for about 2 minutes. The skins should turn light golden brown, but be careful not to scorch them.

5 When done, remove from skillet and place on paper towels on a plate to remove excess oil.

6 When cool, cut each roll at an angle into 3 pieces and serve with the dipping sauce.

7 To make the sauce, stir the liquid ingredients in a mixing bowl until well blended, then stir in the remaining ingredients and serve.

Serves 4
Preparation time: **15 mins**
Cooking time: **10 mins**

Chinese-style Eggplant Salad

1 lb (450 g) Asian
  eggplants
Fresh coriander leaves
  (cilantro) to garnish
  (optional)

Dressing
6 cloves fresh garlic,
  finely minced
1 teaspoon soy sauce
2 teaspoons vinegar
$^1/_2$ teaspoon salt
1 teaspoon sugar
$^1/_2$ teaspoon freshly
  ground black pepper
1 tablespoon sesame oil

1 Bring a large pot of water to a rolling boil, and add
the whole eggplants. Let water return to the boil,
reduce the heat to low, and cook until the eggplants
change color and become tender, about 8 minutes.
2 Drain eggplants in a colander. When cool enough
to handle, cut eggplants in half lengthways, then cut
each half into 2-in (5-cm) long pieces, and place in a
mixing bowl.
3 Stir together all dressing ingredients, except sesame
oil. Using a whisk or fork, beat in the sesame oil until
well blended. Pour the dressing evenly over the eggplants and toss to blend. Transfer to a serving dish.
Garnish with coriander leaves if desired.

Serves 4
Preparation time: 10 mins
Cooking time: 8 mins

Tangy Okra Salad

30 pieces okra, washed and drained
Fresh basil or Chinese celery leaf to garnish (optional)

Dressing
6 cloves garlic, finely minced
1 teaspoon fresh ginger, grated
$1/_2$ teaspoon salt
1 teaspoon sugar
2 teaspoon vinegar
1 teaspoon soy sauce
2 tablespoons sesame oil

1 Bring a large pot of water to a rolling boil, and add the okra. Return to the boil, cover, and reduce heat to low. Cook for 3 to 4 minutes, until the okra turns a shiny dark green. Remove from heat and drain well in a colander.

2 To make the dressing, place all ingredients, except the sesame oil, in a small bowl. Slowly dribble in the sesame oil while beating continuously with a whisk or a fork until the dressing is well blended.

3 Arrange the cooked okra on a serving platter, then pour the dressing evenly over them, add garnish if desired, and serve.

Serves 4
Preparation time: 10 mins
Cooking time: 15 mins

Indian Green Bean and Plantain Salad

$^3/_4$ lb (325 g) plantain or pumpkin, peeled and cubed (about 2 cups)
$^1/_2$ lb (225 g) green beans cut into 2-in (5-cm) pieces (about 2 cups)
1 teaspoon ground turmeric
1 teaspoon salt
3 cups (750 ml) water
1 cup (100 g) grated fresh coconut
1 tablespoon ground cumin
2 green chilies
4 sprigs curry leaves
$^1/_2$ cup (125 ml) yogurt
2 tablespoons oil
1 teaspoon mustard seeds

1 Combine plantain or pumpkin cubes, long beans, turmeric, salt, and water in a large saucepan and cook until the plantain is soft.

2 Meanwhile, grind grated coconut, cumin, green chilies, half the curry leaves and yogurt together in a blender until smooth and set aside.

3 Heat oil in a skillet. Fry the mustard seeds until they splutter, then add the curry leaves. When aromatic, transfer to the boiling vegetables along with the blended spices. Boil for 2 minutes, remove from the heat and serve.

Serves 4–6
Preparation time: **20 mins**
Cooking time: **20 mins**

Marinated Chinese Cucumber Salad

$^2/_3$ lb (300 g) baby
  cucumber or gherkin
3 to 4 cloves garlic,
  peeled and crushed

Sauce
2 tablespoons soy sauce
1 tablespoon sesame oil
1 teaspoon vinegar
1 teaspoon sugar
$^1/_2$ teaspoon salt
$^1/_2$ teaspoon freshly
  ground black pepper

1 Wash cucumbers well, pat dry and place on cutting board. Use the side of a cleaver or large knife to press on the cucumbers so they crack open, then cut into 1-in ($2^1/_2$-cm) sections. Place in a large bowl and add the garlic.
2 Combine the sauce ingredients and drizzle evenly over the cucumbers and garlic. Toss well to blend flavors.
3 Cover with plastic wrap and let marinate in the refrigerator for 1 to 2 hours, or for 30 minutes at room temperature. Transfer to a smaller bowl and serve.

Serves 4
Preparation time: **10 mins**
Assembling time: **2 mins**

Malaysian-style Eggs with Spicy Chili Paste

4 to 5 dried chilies
4 fresh red chilies, seeds and pith discarded
6 shallots, chopped
4 tablespoons oil
2 teaspoons lime or lemon juice
1 to $1^1/_2$ teaspoons sugar
1 teaspoon salt
4 hard-boiled eggs, shelled

Serves 4
Preparation time: **15 mins**
Cooking time: **20 mins**

1 Cut dried chilies into $^3/_4$-in ($1^1/_2$-cm) lengths and remove seeds. Soak in warm water until soft, 10 to 15 minutes. Drain chilies and discard water and seeds.

2 Process soaked chilies, fresh chilies, and shallots to a smooth paste in a blender, adding oil, if needed.

3 Heat oil in a wok over medium heat and add ground ingredients. Stir-fry until chili paste is cooked and oil separates, about 10 minutes.

4 Stir in lime juice, sugar, and salt to taste.

5 Cut eggs in half lengthwise. Place on a serving dish and spoon the cooked chili paste over the eggs.

Gujarati Green Bean Salad

1 cup (250 ml) water
³/₄ lb (350 g) green
  beans, sliced (about
  3 cups)
2 tablespoons oil
1 teaspoon mustard seeds
1 medium onion, peeled
  and thinly sliced
2 green chilies, seeded
  and thinly sliced
¹/₂ teaspoon salt
1 teaspoon sugar
1 cup (100 g) fresh
  grated coconut
¹/₂ cup (70 g) roasted
  peanuts, ground

1 Bring water to a boil in a pan. Add the beans and return to the boil. Cook for 1 minute. Remove from heat, drain the beans, and rinse in cold water. Set aside in a mixing bowl.

2 Heat oil in a separate pan. Add the mustard seeds and fry until they splutter.

3 Add onion and chilies and sauté for 1 minute, or until the onion softens.

4 Remove from the heat and combine with the beans, add all the remaining ingredients, and mix well. Serve with rice.

Serves 4
Preparation time: 20 mins
Cooking time: 10 mins

Thai Spicy Corn Kernel Salad

^{1}/$_2$ cup (50 g) fresh grated coconut

5 to 6 corn cobs, or two 13-oz (415 g) cans of corn kernels, drained

1 cup (250 ml) water

^{1}/$_2$ tablespoon Thai chili paste (*nam prik pao*)

2 tablespoons soy sauce

2 tablespoons lime or lemon juice

1 teaspoon sugar

^{1}/$_4$ cup (50 g) roasted peanuts, coarsely ground

^{1}/$_4$ cup (60 ml) coconut milk

2 sprigs fresh coriander leaves (cilantro), coarsely chopped

1 Roast the coconut at 350°F (180°C) until golden brown, stirring often, about 10 minutes. Alternatively, dry roast the grated coconut in a skillet over low heat, about 10 minutes, until golden brown.

2 Steam or boil corn cobs until tender, around 6 to 8 minutes. Set aside to cool. Once cool, cut the kernels from the cobs. If using canned corn, heat the corn kernels in the water over medium heat until hot, about 10 minutes. Drain and set aside.

3 In a large mixing bowl, combine all the ingredients and stir well. Serve on individual plates or arrange in a large serving bowl.

Serves 4 to 6
Preparation time: **10 mins**
Cooking time: **20 mins**

Thai Grilled Eggplant Salad

8 oz (225 g) firm tofu
$^1/_2$ teaspoon salt
1 cup (250 ml) oil
1 lb (450 g) Asian
  eggplants
$^1/_2$ cup (100 g) red
  onion, thinly sliced
1 small chili, coarsely
  chopped (optional)

Dressing
1 tablespoon fresh lime
  or lemon juice
2 teaspoons soy sauce
1 teaspoon sugar

1 Sprinkle both sides of the tofu with salt. Heat oil in a wok or saucepan and deep-fry the tofu until golden brown on both sides. Drain on paper towels and cut into 1-in ($2^1/_2$-cm) cubes. Cool to room temperature and set aside.

2 Score the eggplant lengthwise with the tip of a knife. Grill or broil until soft, about 10 minutes. When cool enough to handle, peel the eggplants and cut into 2-in (5-cm) long pieces. Arrange the slices on a serving platter.

3 Combine the dressing ingredients and pour over the eggplants before serving and garnish with the onion, chilies, and fried tofu cubes.

Serves 4
Preparation time: **15 mins**
Cooking time: **10 mins**

Steamed Pumpkin Salad with Chinese Sesame Vinaigrette

1 lb (450 g) pumpkin, peeled, seeded and cut into wedges
2 oz (60 g) dried glass noodles
1 cup (200 g) bell peppers, thinly sliced
3 teaspoons sesame seeds, roasted and coarsely ground
Chili oil for garnish (optional)

Dressing
3 teaspoons soy sauce
2 teaspoon vinegar
$^1/_2$ teaspoon freshly ground black pepper
$^1/_2$ teaspoon salt
$^1/_2$ to 1 teaspoon sugar
2 teaspoons sesame oil

1 Place a steamer rack in a saucepan. Arrange pumpkin on a heatproof plate and set on rack. Cover steamer tightly and steam pumpkin over medium heat for 25 minutes. Remove the pumpkin from steamer. When cool enough to handle, cut pumpkin into thin strips $^1/_4$ to $^1/_2$ in ($^1/_2$ to 1 cm) thick. Set aside.

2 Soak glass noodles in hot water for 10 to 15 minutes until soft and drain.

3 Stir together all dressing ingredients, except sesame oil. Using a whisk or fork, beat in the sesame oil until well blended.

4 Place the pumpkin wedges and bell pepper slices in a large salad bowl. Stir the dressing again to blend, and pour over the vegetables. Toss until vegetables are completely coated with the dressing.

5 Transfer to a smaller serving dish, sprinkle with ground sesame seeds, and drizzle with chili oil, if desired.

Serves 4–6
Preparation time: 35 mins
Cooking time: 40 mins

Indonesian Vegetable Salad with Peanut Dressing

8 oz (225 g) firm tofu
1/2 teaspoon salt
1 cup (250 ml) oil
2 cups (350 g) cucumber, sliced
1 1/3 cups (200 g) cabbage, thinly shredded
10 Boston lettuce leaves, coarsely sliced or torn
2 medium potatoes, boiled, and cut in wedges
3 hard-boiled eggs, shelled and sliced
Deep-fried melinjo nut wafers (*krupuk emping*) or vegetable crackers or unsalted potato chips

Peanut Dressing
3 red chilies, seeds removed and sliced
2 teaspoons fresh galangal, grated
4 cloves garlic
3 kaffir lime leaves, blanched in boiling water to soften, sliced
1/4 cup tamarind juice (see page 7)
2 teaspoons salt
1/2 cup (90 g) palm sugar, finely chopped or crumbled
1 1/2 cups (250 g) peanuts, dry roasted
2 cups (500 ml) hot water

1 Sprinkle both sides of the tofu with salt. Heat oil in a wok or saucepan and deep-fry the tofu until golden brown on both sides. Drain on paper towels and cut into 1-in (2 1/2-cm) cubes. Cool to room temperature.
2 To prepare the peanut dressing, process the chilies, galangal, garlic, lime leaves, tamarind juice, salt and palm sugar in a spice grinder or blender until smooth. Grind peanuts coarsely in a food processor. Add spice paste and pulse a couple of times. Add water and pulse to make a thick sauce.
3 Put the tofu, cucumber, cabbage, lettuce and potatoes in a large bowl. Add the dressing and toss to mix thoroughly. Transfer to a serving dish and top with sliced egg and nut wafers.

*Deep-fried **melinjo nut wafers** are available in packets. They have a fragrant "nutty" flavor with a slightly bitter aftertaste.*

Serves 4
Preparation time: **15 mins**
Cooking time: **30 mins**

Spicy Indonesian Coconut Salad

$^1/_2$ lb (225 g) bean
  sprouts, rinsed and
  cleaned, seed casings
  removed
1 cup (150 g) green
  beans, cut into 2-in (5-
  cm) lengths
1 cup (150 g) cabbage,
  thinly sliced
2 cups (150 g) green
  leafy Asian vegetable
  such as bok choy or
  choy sum
2 cups (150 g) water
  convolvulus (*kangkong*),
  coarsely chopped

Coconut Dressing
2 red chilies, seeds
  removed
3 cloves garlic
2 teaspoons fresh
  galangal or fresh
  ginger, grated
$^1/_2$ teaspoon ground
  coriander seeds
3 kaffir lime leaves, sliced
1 tablespoon palm sugar
  shaved or finely chopped
1 teaspoon salt
2 cups (200 g) grated
  fresh coconut

1 Place all coconut dressing ingredients except the
coconut in the food processor and process. Transfer
to a heatproof bowl and stir in the coconut. Put bowl
in a steamer, cover and cook over boiling water for
30 minutes. Transfer to a wide container and set aside
to cool.
2 Blanch the vegetables separately. Drain all the vegetables and place in a large bowl. Add the coconut
dressing and toss. Serve at room temperature.

Serves 4
Preparation time: **20 mins**
Cooking time: **45 mins**

Chinese Lotus Root Salad
with Sesame Dressing

$^1/_2$ lb (225 g) fresh lotus
 root, washed
$^1/_3$ lb (150 g) green
 beans, trimmed
 and halved
1 teaspoon salt
1 medium carrot, peeled
 and sliced
$^1/_2$ cup (80 g) fresh or
 frozen green peas
1 large stalk celery,
 stringy fibers removed,
 and diced

Dressing
3 tablespoons vegetarian
 mushroom oyster sauce
2 cloves garlic, minced
1 teaspoon sesame oil
2 teaspoons sesame
 paste or tahini
$^1/_2$ teaspoon salt

Serves 4
Preparation time: 30 mins
Cooking time: 50 mins

1 Place lotus roots in a pot and add 8 cups (2 liters) water. Bring to a full boil, cover, reduce the heat to low, and cook for 40 minutes. Remove from the heat, drain lotus roots, and set stock aside. Rinse the lotus roots in cool water, drain, and set aside to cool. When cool enough to handle, cut lotus roots into round slices about $^1/_4$ in (6 mm) thick.
2 Bring the lotus stock to the boil and blanch the beans until they turn dark and shiny. Remove from the heat, drain, and rinse beans in cool water. Drain and set beans aside to cool. Discard stock.
3 Bring a saucepan of water with the salt to the boil. Add the carrots and cook for 3 minutes; remove with slotted spoon, rinse and set aside. Add the peas and celery, and cook for 1 minute; remove with slotted spoon, rinse, and set aside.
4 In a large salad bowl, combine the dressing ingredients, stirring well. Add all the vegetables and toss together until well mixed. Transfer to a smaller salad bowl or platter and serve.

Jicama can be used as a substitute if lotus root is not available. Cut into bite-sized pieces and blanch in hot water or eat raw if young and tender.

Dry Noodles with Sesame and Garlic Dressing

This traditional and very tasty form of Chinese "fast food" is quick and easy to prepare. You may apply the recipe to virtually any type of noodle, adjust the sauce to your own taste, and add whatever sort of vegetables you like best. Works great as a salad or appetizer!

1 teaspoon salt
8 oz (250 g) dried wheat
  or other noodles
1 handful fresh mung
  bean sprouts, washed
  and drained
1 red bell pepper, seeded
  and julienned
2 scallions, minced
Freshly ground black
  pepper to taste

Dressing
2 tablespoons sesame
  paste or tahini, blended
  with 3 teaspoons water
1 teaspoon vinegar
$1/_2$ teaspoon salt
$1^1/_2$ teaspoons sugar
1 teaspoon vegetarian
  mushroom oyster sauce
1 teaspoon soy sauce
1 tablespoon olive oil
2 cloves garlic, minced

1 In a large mixing bowl, stir together the dressing ingredients, and add garlic.
2 Bring a large pot of water with salt to a boil, and cook the noodles according to package directions.
3 Drain the noodles, rinse under cool water, and drain again. Place noodles in a large bowl. Add dressing and mix well. Toss in the bean sprouts and red bell pepper. Garnish with scallions and ground black pepper.

Serves 4
Preparation time: **10 mins**
Cooking time: **8 mins**

Sichuan Noodles with Chili Oil

In addition to its delicious taste, this dish delivers a rich parcel of nutritional and medicinal benefits. The sauce contains sesame paste, which is an excellent source of essential fatty acids and benefits bowel functions. Ground peanuts provide a quick source of energy, and Sichuan pepper assists digestion and assimilation of nutrients. The recipe uses ordinary dried wheat noodles that may be purchased in any Asian grocery, but you may also use fresh noodles, as well as rice, buckwheat, egg, or any other type of noodle you wish.

10 oz (300 g) dried
  wheat noodles
1 teaspoon sesame oil
1 tablespoon coarsely
  ground roast peanuts
2 scallions, finely sliced

Sauce
3 teaspoons sesame
  paste or tahini
$2/_3$ cup (165 ml) water
3 teaspoons thick soy
  sauce
1 teaspoon sugar
$1/_2$ teaspoon ground
  Sichuan pepper
2 teaspoons red chili oil
1 teaspoon vinegar

1 To mix the sauce, place sesame paste in the bottom of a bowl and slowly pour in the water while whisking continuously. Add the soy sauce, sugar and ground Sichuan pepper, while stirring continuously, then add the chili oil and vinegar, and blend well.

2 Bring a large pot of water to a boil, add the dried noodles and cook according to package directions.

3 Drain noodles in a colander, rinse in cold water, drain, place in a large bowl then drizzle on 1 teaspoon sesame oil and mix well.

4 Add the sauce to the noodles and toss to mix well, then sprinkle on the ground peanuts and chopped scallions.

5 Serve in a large serving dish at the table, or distribute equally into individual noodle bowls and serve.

Serves 4
Preparation time: 5 mins
Cooking time: 5 mins

Nourishing Chinese Green Pea and Tofu Soup

Black moss fungus or "angel hair" is known in China for its blood-building properties and as a tonic food that turns grey hair black again. Here, it's combined with soft tofu and green peas to make a tasty, nourishing soup.

4 cups (1 liter) vegetarian soup stock or water
$1/_2$ teaspoon salt
1 medium carrot, peeled and diced
1 cake soft tofu (about 8 oz or 225 g), cubed
$1/_2$ cup (50 g) fresh *shiitake* mushrooms, diced or 5 pieces dried *shiitake*, washed and soaked in hot water for 10 minutes and diced
$1/_2$ cup (80 g) fresh or frozen green peas
1 handful dried black moss fungus, washed and soaked 10 minutes in cool water
3 teaspoons cornstarch stirred in 3 tablespoons cool water (optional)
2 teaspoons sesame oil
2 scallions, chopped, for garnish

1 Bring the stock or water and the salt to a full boil, and add the diced carrot and tofu. Cover, reduce heat to medium, and cook for 3 minutes.

2 Add the mushrooms, peas, and fungus to the soup, cover, and cook for another 2 minutes.

3 Stir the cornstarch mixture into the soup and it will thicken as it comes to the boil. Drizzle in the sesame oil, stir, and turn off heat. Ladle into individual bowls, add the scallions, and serve.

This soup goes well with a dash of ground black pepper or Sichuan peppercorn. Another nice embellishment is to add a small handful of very fresh mung bean sprouts to each serving bowl before ladling in the soup; this adds both fresh flavor and a pleasant crunch to the texture. If black moss fungus is not available, use $1/_2$ cup glass noodles, soaked in hot water for 10 minutes to soften.

Serves 4
Preparation time: **5 mins + 10 mins soaking time**
Cooking time: **20 mins**

Kerala Vegetable Stew

2 tablespoons oil
2 tablespoons split chickpeas (*channa dal*)
2 tablespoons black
  lentils (*urad dal*)
2 green chilies, seeded
  and chopped
10 cloves garlic, sliced
1 1/2 tablespoons cumin
  seeds
1/2 cup (50 g) grated
  fresh coconut
1 teaspoon ground
  turmeric
1 cup (250 ml) water
1 cup (100 g) cabbage,
  sliced
3/4 cup (100 g) carrots,
  sliced
1 cup (50 g) green
  beans, cut into 1-in
  (2 1/2-cm) pieces
2 cups (250 g) cauli-
  flower, cut into small
  florets
1 cup (100 g) green peas
1 1/4 teaspoons salt
2 cups (500 ml) water
2 tablespoons ghee or
  butter or vegetable oil
1 teaspoon cumin seeds
1 teaspoon mustard seeds
2 sprigs curry leaves

1 Heat oil in a wok over medium heat and fry chick-peas and black lentils until golden brown. Add the green chilies, garlic, cumin seeds, grated coconut, and turmeric. Sauté until coconut is a shade darker, about 5 minutes.

2 Cool the stir-fried ingredients and blend with 1 cup water until smooth.

3 Put all the vegetables, salt, and the water into a pan with the blended ingredients and cook over medium heat for about 15 minutes.

4 In a separate pan, heat the ghee or butter or oil over medium heat, and fry the cumin and mustard seeds, and the curry leaves until the mustard seeds splutter.

5 Transfer to the vegetable stew. Continue to simmer for about 5 minutes, then turn off heat.

Serves 6
Preparation time: 25 mins
Cooking time: 30 mins

Spicy Indian Lentil Stew

$^{1}/_{2}$ cup (100 g) split
  yellow lentils (*tur dal*),
  washed and drained
$^{1}/_{4}$ cup (50 g) split mung
  beans (*mung dal*),
  washed and drained
$^{1}/_{4}$ cup (50 g) split red
  lentils (*masoor dal*),
  washed and drained
4 teaspoons ghee or oil
5 cups (1$^{1}/_{4}$ liters) water
1 teaspoon ground
  turmeric
1$^{1}/_{4}$ teaspoons salt
1 teaspoon cumin seeds
1 medium onion, thinly
  sliced
2 green chilies, seeded
  and cut into thick slices
2 teaspoons fresh ginger,
  grated
2 tablespoons fresh
  coriander leaves
  (cilantro), chopped
$^{1}/_{2}$ teaspoon cayenne
  pepper
1 tablespoon lemon juice

1 Place the yellow lentils, split mung beans and split red lentils in a saucepan with 1 teaspoon ghee, water, turmeric, and salt. Bring to the boil and cook for about 30 minutes.

2 Remove from heat and, using the back of a wooden spoon, mash the lentils and beans.

3 Heat 3 teaspoons ghee in a separate pan. Add cumin seeds, cook them until they splutter, and add the onion, chilies, and ginger. Stir-fry until the onions are soft, and add the coriander leaves and cayenne pepper. Stir to mix well and transfer to the mashed lentils and beans.

4 Return to the boil and cook for 3 minutes. Remove from heat and stir in the lemon juice. Serve with rice.

Serves 4–6
Preparation time: **15 mins**
Cooking time: **45 mins**

Mixed Vegetables and Noodles in Broth

This recipe may also be prepared with any sort of leafy vegetables, as well as various types of noodles — for example, its excellent with rice or mung bean vermicelli. Simply follow the label directions for preparing the noodles, then add to the soup.

3 large dried *shiitake* mushrooms, soaked in hot water for 20 minutes
6 cups (1$^1/_2$ liters) vegetable stock or water
1 tablespoon Chinese wolfberries (optional)
2 teaspoons salt
2 teaspoons soy sauce
1 teaspoon sugar
1 cup (120 g) fresh lotus root, thinly sliced (optional)
$^3/_4$ cup (140 g) pickled bamboo shoots, blanched and drained, halved lengthwise and thinly sliced
5 oz (150 g) dried wheat noodles, any variety
2 cups (100 g) bok choy, sliced into 2$^1/_2$ in (6 cm) lengths
2 teaspoons sesame oil

Serves 4
Preparation time: 10 mins
+ 20 mins soaking time
Cooking time: 40 mins

1 Drain soaked mushrooms, cut them in half, and reserve soaking liquid. Set aside.
2 Bring the vegetable stock or water to the boil in a large pot. Add wolfberry and *shiitake*, cover, and cook for 1 to 2 minutes.
3 Add salt, soy sauce, and sugar, then add lotus root and bamboo shoots. Cover, reduce heat to low, and cook for 3 to 4 minutes. Remove from the heat and set aside, covered.
4 Bring a large pot of water to a boil, and cook the noodles according to package directions.
5 Remove and drain the noodles, rinse under cool water, and add noodles to the soup pot together with the bok choy. Bring the soup to the boil, and remove from the heat.
6 Stir in the sesame oil, and transfer to soup tureen or ladle into individual serving bowls.

Chinese wolfberries, also known as Chinese boxthorns or matrimony vines, are available from Chinese medicine or grocery stores. Dried cranberries or other small, taut berries may be substituted. Bamboo shoots are available fresh at some Chinese markets, and can be stored in a refrigerator. Canned bamboo shoots are more widely available and should be rinsed well before use. Dried bamboo shoots are also available, while pickled bamboo shoots are regarded as a delicacy in some Asian countries.

South Indian-style Thick Yogurt Soup

$^1/_4$ cup (50 g) split mung beans (*mung dal*)

5 cups (1$^1/_4$ liters) water

2 medium ripe tomatoes, chopped

1 teaspoon ground turmeric

1 teaspoon ground cumin

5 cloves garlic, finely minced

1 teaspoon freshly ground black pepper

2 tablespoons oil

$^1/_2$ teaspoon mustard seeds

2 dried chilies, seeded and cut into 1-in (2$^1/_2$-cm) pieces

1 teaspoon cumin seeds

$^1/_4$ teaspoon fenugreek

2 sprigs curry leaves

1$^1/_4$ teaspoons salt

1 cup (250 ml) yogurt mixed with $^1/_2$ cup (125 ml) water

1 Place split mung beans, water, tomatoes, turmeric, and cumin in a pot, bring to the boil over medium heat, and cook until the beans are very soft, about 15 minutes. Remove from heat.

2 Using a sieve, strain the liquid into a bowl and set aside. Mash the cooked beans thoroughly, then put mashed beans and soup back into the pot.

3 Season with garlic and pepper. Return to the boil and cook over medium heat for about 10 minutes.

4 Heat the oil in a separate pan and fry the mustard seeds, dried chilies, cumin seeds, fenugreek, and curry leaves until aromatic and the dried chilies turn brown. Then remove from the heat. Transfer to the simmering soup.

5 Add salt, pour in the yogurt, and mix well. Remove from the heat as it begins to boil.

Serves 4–6
Preparation time: **15 mins**
Cooking time: **20 mins**

Chinese Spinach, Mushroom and Tofu in Clear Broth

1 tablespoon vegetable oil
2 cloves garlic, peeled and crushed
2 slices fresh ginger
10 oz (300 g) fresh spinach, washed and trimmed
3 1/4 cups (800 ml) vegetable stock or water
1 cake soft tofu (about 8 oz or 225 g), cubed
1 cup (100 g) fresh button or *shiitake* mushrooms,
2 teaspoons sesame oil
Salt and freshly ground black pepper to taste

1 Heat oil in a wok until smoking, add the garlic and ginger, and stir-fry for 30 seconds. Add the spinach and stir-fry for about 2 minutes.

2 Add the vegetable stock, tofu, and button mushrooms, and cover the wok. Bring to a full boil, reduce heat to low, and cook for 2 to 3 minutes.

3 Remove from the heat, stir in sesame oil, salt and pepper to taste, and serve.

Serves 4
Preparation time: **10 mins**
Cooking time: **10 mins**

Spicy Thai Tofu Salad with Mushrooms

10 fresh mushrooms
1 lb (450 g) firm tofu, diced
1/4 cup (60 ml) fresh lime or lemon juice
2 tablespoons soy sauce
1/2 teaspoon salt
1/2 teaspoon sugar
3 tablespoons roasted rice powder (see note)
1 small chili, seeded and minced
1 scallion, minced
2 shallots, thinly sliced
2 tablespoons fresh coriander leaves (cilantro), chopped
1/2 cup (10 g) fresh mint leaves, chopped

1 Steam mushrooms for 5 minutes and slice.
2 Combine the tofu with the mushrooms in a bowl. Mix the lime juice, soy sauce, salt and sugar, and stir into the tofu and mushrooms. Stir in the rice powder, chilies, scallion, shallots, coriander, and mint leaves.
3 Arrange the tofu mixture on a serving platter and surround with vegetables such as lettuce leaves, cabbage leaves, sliced cucumbers, and green beans, as desired.

*To make **roasted rice powder**, dry-roast 1/2 cup (120 g) raw Thai jasmine or long-grain rice in a skillet over medium heat, stirring constantly until light brown, then grind with a pestle and mortar, or in a food processor. Store in an airtight container.*

Serves 4 to 6
Preparation time: **10 mins**
Cooking time: **10 mins**

'Crinkle-fried' Dried Tofu

This recipe employs a traditional Sichuan cooking technique called *gan bian* ("crinkle-fry"), in which the main ingredient is continuously stir-fried in a small amount of oil over medium heat until it starts to "crinkle," such as in the famous Sichuan dish, "crinkle-fried green beans."

3 tablespoons oil
1 teaspoon salt
9 oz (280 g) dried tofu, cut into $1/2$ in x $1^1/_2$ in (1 cm x $3^1/_2$ cm) strips (about 3 cups)
1 medium carrot, shredded
1 teaspoon vinegar
1 teaspoon sesame oil
$1/_2$ cup (20 g) fresh Chinese celery or coriander leaves (cilantro), coarsely chopped

Sauce
3 teaspoons hoisin sauce
1 teaspoon sugar
3 teaspoons rice wine
2 teaspoons soy sauce

1 Heat oil in a wok until hot but not smoking. Add 1 teaspoon salt to the hot oil, and stir in the dried tofu sticks. Stir-fry continuously over medium heat until the tofu starts to crinkle and turn crispy, about 15 minutes. Remove with slotted spoon and set aside on a plate.

2 In the remaining oil, stir-fry the carrot for 30 seconds, and add the sauce ingredients. Cook for 1 minute more, then add the fried tofu sticks. Stir-fry 1 minute, ensuring that tofu sticks are coated in the sauce. Add vinegar and stir-fry 30 seconds more. Turn off the heat, add sesame oil, and toss to combine.

3 Transfer to a serving plate, garnish with the chopped celery leaves, and serve.

Serves 4
Preparation time: **10 mins**
Cooking time: **25 mins**

Steamed Tofu with *Shiitake* Mushrooms

10-oz (300 g) soft tofu
5 dried *shiitake* mushrooms, soaked in hot water for 20 minutes, stems removed and finely diced
3 pieces dried wood ear fungus, soaked in hot water for 20 minutes and minced
5 cloves garlic, minced
5 slices fresh ginger, minced
6 scallions, minced
Chopped celery leaves or fresh coriander leaves (cilantro) for garnish

Seasonings
1 teaspoon salt
1 teaspoon sugar
1 teaspoon soy sauce
1 tablespoon rice wine
$1/2$ teaspoon freshly ground black pepper
2 tablespoons sesame oil

1 Heat water in a steamer pan with rack and bring to a boil.

2 Meanwhile, wash the tofu, drain well, and pat dry with paper towels (or let tofu drain on rack for one hour before preparation). Using fingers, crumble and mash the tofu into one medium heatproof bowl or four individual serving bowls (as shown).

3 Stir seasonings into the mashed tofu. Add diced mushrooms, wood ears, garlic, ginger, and scallions. Stir until evenly blended.

4 Set the bowl(s) of tofu mixture on the steaming rack, cover steamer tightly, and cook for 20 minutes. Remove bowl from steamer, set onto a plate, and garnish with chopped celery leaves or fresh coriander leaves before serving.

Serves 4
Preparation time: 20 mins
Cooking time: 25 mins

Sichuanese 'Numb Hot' Stir-fried Tofu

2 tablespoons oil

3 slices fresh ginger, minced

2 cloves garlic, minced

$1/2$ cup (125 ml) water

14 oz (400 g) firm tofu, cubed

1 cup (160 g) fresh or frozen mixed vegetables, such as peas, corn, and diced carrots

6 dried *shiitake* mushrooms, soaked in hot water for 15 to 20 minutes, drained and diced

1 teaspoon ground Sichuan pepper

$1/2$ teaspoon freshly ground black pepper

1 teaspoon cornstarch mixed with 1 tablespoon water

1 scallion, minced

1 small red chili, thinly sliced

1 teaspoon sesame oil

Sauce

3 teaspoons hoisin sauce

$1/2$ teaspoon sugar

1 teaspoon soy sauce

2 teaspoons rice wine

1 Combine the sauce ingredients in a bowl and set aside.

2 Heat the oil in a wok over medium-high heat until smoking and add the minced ginger and garlic. Stir-fry 10 seconds.

3 Add the sauce, stir a few times, add the water, and stir again to blend. When sauce comes to a boil, add the tofu, mixed vegetables, and mushrooms and stir-fry. Cover, reduce heat to medium, and cook for 7 to 8 minutes.

4 Add the Sichuan and black pepper, stirring to blend. Cover and simmer 1 more minute before adding the cornstarch mixture. Stir until sauce thickens and bring to the boil again.

5 Remove from heat, stir in the scallion, chili, and sesame oil, and serve.

Serves 4
Preparation time: **5 mins**
Cooking time: **15 mins**

Stir-fried Tofu and Roasted Peanuts

This is a tasty, lively dish with firm and crunchy textures and plenty of spice. It goes well with rice, and could also be used as a stuffing for various wraps, such as Chinese pancakes, seaweed sheets, or whole leaves of iceberg lettuce.

Sauce
2 tablespoons fermented black bean sauce
1 teaspoon sugar
2 teaspoons rice wine
1 tablespoon water

2 tablespoons oil
1–2 fresh red chilies, halved lengthwise, seeded, and minced
3 cloves garlic, minced
2 slices fresh ginger, minced
1 scallion, minced
1/2 head cabbage, cut into 3/4-in (2-cm) squares
2 cakes dried tofu, cubed
1/3 cup (65 g) roasted peanuts, shells and skins removed
1 small stalk fresh celery, tough fibers removed and diced

1 Combine the sauce ingredients in a bowl and set aside.
2 Heat the oil in a wok over high heat until very hot, and stir-fry the chili, garlic, ginger, and scallion. Add the cabbage and tofu. Stir-fry for 1 minute.
3 Add the sauce and continue to cook for 4 to 5 minutes.
4 Add the peanuts, stir-fry 30 seconds more or until peanuts are heated through, and remove from the heat. Place in a serving dish, garnish with the diced celery, and serve.

Dried tofu is another variety of firm tofu. It usually comes in the form of a small rectangular block and is bright yellow. Substitute with firm tofu if unavailable.

Serves 4
Preparation time: 20 mins
Cooking time: 10 mins

Claypot-braised Chinese Tofu and Vegetables

For best results, prepare this dish in a traditional Chinese clay pot, which is designed to allow all the seasoning flavors to blend slowly and completely. A normal casserole pot can also be used, however.

4 cups (1 liter) water
Two 8-in (20-cm) pieces
   dried *konbu*
2 teaspoons rice wine
10 oz (300 g) soft
   tofu, cubed
1 *daikon*, peeled, cut
   lengthwise and sliced
   thinly at an angle
1 medium carrot, cut
   lengthwise and sliced
   thinly at an angle
6 button mushrooms,
   wiped clean and cut
   into 3 pieces each
1 canned bamboo shoot,
   washed, drained, and
   thinly sliced
1 cup (200 g) white
   or yellow onions,
   peeled and cut into
   thin crescents
1 teaspoon sugar
2 teaspoons salt
2 teaspoons soy sauce
20 fresh snow peas,
   tops, tails, and central
   rib removed
1 fresh red chili, halved
   lengthways
2 teaspoons sesame oil

1 Put 4 cups water, the *konbu*, and rice wine into a clay pot. Bring to the boil, reduce the heat to low, cover, and cook for 20 minutes.
2 Add the tofu, *daikon*, carrot, mushrooms, bamboo shoot, and onions. Stir in the sugar, salt, and soy sauce, cover, and cook for another 10 minutes.
3 Add the snow peas and chilies, cooking for 1 more minute. Remove from the heat.
4 Drizzle in the sesame oil, mixing well, and serve.

Serves 4
Preparation time: **30 mins**
Cooking time: **45 mins**

Malaysian-style Stuffed Tofu

An alternative presentation of this dish is to dice the deep-fried tofu, arrange it on a plate, and scatter with the shredded vegetables and bean sprouts.

4 cakes firm tofu, about
  1 1/4 lb (600 g)
Salt to taste
1 cup (250 ml) oil
1/2 cup (70 g) finely
  shredded jicama
1/2 cup (70 g) finely
  shredded cucumber
1 cup (80 g) bean
  sprouts, blanched for
  about 1 minute

Chili Sauce
2 red chilies, seeded and
  minced
2 cloves garlic, minced
1/2 teaspoon salt
1 tablespoon sugar
3 tablespoons water
2 tablespoons vinegar
2 tablespoons tomato
  ketchup

1 Halve each piece of tofu diagonally. Pat carefully with paper towels to absorb moisture. Rub some salt over the tofu.

2 To prepare the chili sauce, process chilies, garlic, salt and sugar in a blender until coarsely ground. Add water, vinegar, and tomato ketchup and process until smooth. Put in a sauce bowl.

3 Heat oil in a wok over medium heat and fry the tofu, turning until crisp and golden on all sides, about 4 minutes. Remove and drain on paper towels, and set aside to cool. When cool, make a horizontal slit on the cut side of each piece of tofu to create a pocket, being careful not to cut through.

4 Stuff each tofu pocket with the vegetables and serve with chili sauce.

Serves 4
Preparation time: **20 mins**
Cooking time: **15 mins**

Make a horizontal slit on the cut side of each piece of deep-fried tofu.

Stuff each tofu pocket with the vegetables.

Tofu Braised with Sichuan Seasonings

In this recipe, tofu is combined with dried *shiitake* mushroom, pickled turnips, ginger, scallions, other savory seasonings to produce a dish that warms the body, stimulates digestion, and serenades the palate with a symphony of harmonious taste.

$1/_2$ lb (225 g) bok choy, tough leaves discarderd
$1/_3$ cup (80 ml) plus 2 tablespoons oil
2 cakes firm tofu (about 1 lb or 450 g)
2 slices fresh ginger, julienned
1 scallion, cut into 3 sections
6 large dried *shiitake* mushrooms, soaked in hot water for 20 minutes then drained, tough stems discarded
$1/_4$ cup (30 g) pickled turnips, finely chopped
2 teaspoons cornstarch stirred in 2 tablespoons water

Sauce
2 tablespoons soy sauce
1 teaspoon salt
1 teaspoon sugar
1 tablespoon rice wine
1 teaspoon freshly ground black pepper
1 tablespoon sesame oil

1 Mix the sauce ingredients and set aside.
2 Blanch bok choy for 1 minute, rinse under cold water, drain, and cut each head in half lengthways. Set aside.
3 Heat $1/_3$ cup (80 ml) oil in a wok over high heat until hot but not smoking. Halve and quarter tofu pieces to yield 16 pieces. Add the tofu, and turn with a spatula until light golden. Remove with a slotted spoon and set on a rack or on paper towels to drain. Discard the oil.
4 Heat remaining 2 tablespoons oil in wok until hot but not smoking. Add the ginger, scallion, mushrooms, and pickled turnips, and stir-fry for 2 minutes. Then add the tofu and continue to stir-fry for another 1 to 2 minutes.
5 Stir the sauce, then add to the tofu and stir-fry mixture. For more gravy, add $1/_4$ cup (60 ml) water. Add the cornstarch mixture, stir to blend, cover, and reduce heat to medium. Cook for 6 minutes.
6 Separate bok choy leaves and line the edges of a serving dish with them. Transfer the braised tofu onto the leaves and serve.

Serves 4
Preparation time: **15 mins**
Cooking time: **20 mins**

Red-braised Tofu Steak with Chili Paste

Tofu has long been popular as a meat substitute in China, and has made a big impact in the West, especially when cooked with robust seasonings and fragrant sauces, in order to become palatable and earn its place on the dining table. You may use black bean paste instead of chili sauce and try dusting the cooked steaks with Sichuan pepper-salt for a different taste. This recipe transforms tofu into a "steak" that satisfies as much as any filet mignon — and it's even easier to prepare.

2 cakes firm tofu (about 1 lb or 500 g)
1/4 cup (60 ml) vegetable oil
4 cloves garlic, minced
1 tablespoon chili paste
2 scallions, cut into 1-in (2 1/2-cm) sections

Sauce
1 tablespoon soy sauce
1 tablespoon rice wine
1 teaspoon sesame oil
1 teaspoon sugar
Salt and freshly ground black pepper to taste

Serves 4
Preparation time: **10 mins**
Cooking time: **10 mins**

1 Halve the tofu cakes horizontally to form 4 pieces. Gently press tofu with paper towels to remove excess moisture. Set aside.
2 Mix all sauce ingredients and set aside.
3 Heat the oil in a skillet over high heat until hot but not smoking. Place the tofu in the skillet, and shake the pan gently to prevent sticking. Cook for 2 to 3 minutes, turn carefully with a spatula, and cook the other side for 2 to 3 minutes.
4 Push steaks to side of skillet. Add the garlic and chili paste, stir to blend the flavors and prevent sticking.
5 Add sauce, shake the skillet well to mix all ingredients, cover with lid, reduce heat to low and cook for 2 minutes. Add the scallions, turn tofu over, and cook for 2 minutes. Transfer to a serving dish and season with salt and pepper.

Chinese Homestyle Scrambled Eggs

6 large eggs
1 teaspoon salt
1 teaspoon freshly ground
  black pepper
1 teaspoon sugar
  (optional)
1 teaspoon soy sauce
1 onion, sliced into rings
3 tablespoons oil
3 medium tomatoes
  (about ³/₄ lb or 375 g),
  cut into wedges

1 In a large bowl, beat the eggs well, then add the salt, pepper, sugar, soy sauce, and onion. Continue beating until well blended.

2 Heat the oil in a wok over medium heat and when hot, add the beaten eggs. Scramble the egg mixture quickly with a spatula for 1 to 2 minutes, then add the tomatoes and continue to stir-fry until eggs are uniformly cooked and dry. Transfer to serving dish.

Serves 4
Preparation time: 5 mins
Cooking time: 5 mins

Stir-fried Lotus Root with Scallions

2 fresh lotus roots, about
$^1/_2$ lb (225 g) or $^1/_2$ lb
(225 g) jicama sliced
into $^1/_4$-in ($^1/_2$-cm)
pieces
1 tablespoon oil
2 scallions, thinly sliced
1 teaspoon salt
$^1/_2$ teaspoon sugar
(optional)
$^1/_2$ cup (125 ml) water
1 tablespoon toasted
sesame seeds (optional)

1 Wash the lotus roots well and slice them crosswise into round pieces about $^1/_4$ in ($^1/_2$ cm) thick.
2 Heat the oil in a wok over high heat and when hot, stir-fry the lotus, scallions, salt, and sugar for 2 to 3 minutes.
3 Pour in the water, cover, and reduce heat to medium, cooking for 5 minutes. Transfer to serving dish and garnish with toasted sesame seeds, if desired.

Serves 4
Preparation time: **20 mins**
Cooking time: **10 mins**

Chinese Winter Melon Braised with Ginger

Winter melon has always been a favorite Chinese food, not only for its succulence and fresh flavor, but also for its cooling properties — which soothe the digestive system by counterbalancing the heating properties of meat, chili, garlic, and other ingredients. Winter melon quickly absorbs the taste of whatever seasonings are added to it, so keep the flavorings to a minimum.

3 tablespoons oil
2 in (5 cm) fresh ginger, grated
2 lb (1 kg) winter melon, peeled, seeded and cut into
  1-in (2^1/$_2$-cm) slices
1 teaspoon salt
1 tablespoon sugar
^{1}/$_2$ cup (125 ml) water

1 Heat the oil in a wok over high heat and stir-fry the ginger and winter melon. Continue stir-frying until all the winter melon is coated with oil and the surface begins to soften, 3 to 5 minutes.
2 Add the salt, sugar, and water. Cover the wok, reduce the heat to medium, and cook for about 15 minutes, or until thoroughly tender. Transfer to a serving plate.

Serves 4
Preparation time: **15 mins**
Cooking time: **20 mins**

Sichuan Eggplant Braised in Fragrant Sauce

Chinese cooks usually prepare eggplant with strong seasonings, simmered in richly flavored sauces. This makes these dishes an excellent accompaniment for rice and congee. Leftovers keep well overnight in the refrigerator and may be reheated the next day for lunch.

4 Asian eggplants (about 1 lb or 450 g)
3 tablespoons oil
6 cloves garlic, minced
6 slices fresh ginger, minced
3 scallions, finely chopped
1 tablespoon chili paste
$1/4$ cup (60 ml) water

Sauce
2 tablespoons soy sauce
1 tablespoon rice wine
$1/2$ to 1 tablespoon sugar
1 teaspoon vinegar
$1/2$ teaspoon salt
1 teaspoon sesame oil

1 Halve eggplants lengthways, then cut each half into 2-in (5-cm) long pieces.

2 Combine all the sauce ingredients and set aside.

3 Heat the oil in a wok over high heat and when hot, add the eggplant, garlic and ginger and stir-fry until the eggplant begins to soften, about 4 minutes.

4 Add the scallions and chili paste and cook for 2 minutes. Add the sauce and stir to combine all ingredients. Add water and cover. Reduce heat to low and cook for 5 to 6 minutes. Transfer to a serving dish.

Serves 4
Preparation time: **15 mins**
Cooking time: **35 mins**

Braised Fresh Pumpkin

This is one of the simplest dishes of all to cook, relying entirely on the unadorned rich flavor of pumpkin, which blossoms when allowed to cook in its own juices. Try to select sweet mature pumpkins for this dish. This is a vegetable dish that most children like to eat, which makes it a popular choice for family meals. You may experiment with different flavors, such as adding a cinnamon stick, a sliced vanilla bean or some sliced ginger root to the pot along with the sugar and salt. The finished dish may also be garnished with chopped scallions.

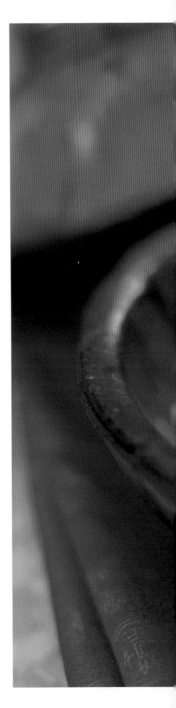

3 tablespoons oil
2 lbs (1 kg) fresh pumpkin, peeled and seeded, cut into 1$^1/_2$ in (3$^1/_2$ cm) chunks
$^1/_2$ to 1 tablespoon sugar
1 teaspoon salt
$^1/_2$ cup (125 ml) water

1 Heat the oil in a large stockpot over medium-low heat. Add the pumpkin and cook, stirring occasionally, until all the pumpkin is coated with oil and begins to soften.
2 Add sugar, salt and water and cover the pot. Reduce the heat to low and cook for about 20 minutes, or until tender, stirring occasionally to prevent sticking. Remove from the heat and serve hot or at room temperature.

Serves 4
Preparation time: 10 mins
Cooking time: 30 mins

Chinese Stir-fried Squash with Fermented Bean Curd

1 1/2 lb (700 g) loofah squash, or summer or yellow squash, peeled
1 tablespoon oil
3 cloves garlic, minced
1 teaspoon fresh ginger, minced
1 teaspoon cornstarch dissolved in 2 tablespoons water
1 scallion, cut into 1-in (2 1/2-cm) lengths, for garnish
1 chili, seeded and sliced for garnish

Sauce
2 squares fermented beancurd (see note)
1/2 teaspoon salt
1 teaspoon sugar
1 teaspoon sesame oil (optional)
1/4 cup (60 ml) water

1 Halve the squash lengthwise. Slice into 1/2-in (1-cm) thick slices at an angle.

2 Combine all the sauce ingredients, stirring to break up the beancurd, then set aside.

3 Heat the oil in a wok until smoking, and stir-fry the garlic and ginger for 30 seconds.

4 Add the squash, stir-fry 1 to 2 minutes, and stir in the sauce. Cover, reduce heat to low, and cook until soft, 4 to 5 minutes, adding more water as it evaporates.

5 Add cornstarch mixture to the squash, stir well, cover, and cook 1 more minute for sauce to thicken. Garnish with scallions and chili.

Fermented beancurd is sold in most Asian markets. The beige-colored cubes are soft and creamy in texture, and taste a little like strong, salty cheese. Available plain or marinated in sesame oil and chili, both types can be used for this recipe.

Serves 4
Preparation time: **10 mins**
Cooking time: **10 mins**

Carrot, *Daikon* and Mushroom Stir-fry

This tasty blend of vegetables, seasoned with fermented bean sauce, provides a wide range of nutrients and medicinal elements, and also provides a very attractive combination of colors and textures. If you prefer, you may use any variety of fresh mushroom in place of the dried shiitake. And if you like a hotter flavour, you may include a teaspoon of your favorite chili paste in the sauce mix. The dish goes well with rice, and may be used as a stuffing for various crêpes and pancakes, nori seaweed wraps, or fresh lettuce leaves.

1/3 cup (85 ml) oil
1 carrot, shredded
1 *daikon*, peeled and shredded
5 large dried *shiitake* mushrooms, soaked in hot water for 20 minutes and thinly sliced
1 leek, green top discarded, sliced into quarters lengthwise, and cut into 1-in (2 1/2-cm) lengths
1 1/2 tablespoons black bean paste
1 tablespoon rice wine
1 teaspoon sugar
2/3 cup (1 bunch) fresh *enokitaki* mushrooms, tough ends removed
2 tablespoons sesame oil
Fresh coriander leaves (cilantro), chopped

1 Heat oil in a wok over high heat until smoking, and stir-fry the carrot, *daikon*, *shiitake*, and leek for 1 minute.

2 Season the vegetables with the bean sauce, wine, and sugar. Reduce heat to medium-high, and cook for 4 to 5 minutes.

3 Add the *enokitaki* mushrooms, stir-fry 1 to 2 minutes more, and stir in the sesame oil. Remove from heat, garnish with chopped coriander, and serve.

Serves 4
Preparation time: **20 mins + 30 mins soaking time**
Cooking time: **10 mins**

Stir-fried Broccoli and Cauliflower with *Shiitake* Mushrooms

6 large dried *shiitake* mushrooms, soaked in hot water 20 minutes
3 cups (750 ml) water
1 head broccoli, cut into florets
1 head cauliflower, cut into florets
1/3 cup (80 ml) oil
4 slices fresh ginger, minced
1 clove garlic, minced
2 scallions, cut into 2-in (5-cm) lengths
1 tablespoon rice wine
2 teaspoons soy sauce
1 teaspoon salt
1 teaspoon sugar
2 teaspoons sesame oil

1 Slice soaked mushrooms into thin strips, and reserve water.
2 Place water in a covered pot and bring to a boil. Add the broccoli and cauliflower florets and let the water return to a full boil. Cook the vegetables for 1 minute, drain in a colander.
3 Heat oil in wok until smoking, and add the ginger, garlic, spring onion and mushrooms. Stir for 1 minute. Add the wine and soy sauce, and stir-fry for 2 minutes.
4 Stir in the vegetables, and season with salt, sugar, sesame oil, and 2 tablespoons of the mushroom soaking water. Cook for 2 more minutes and serve.

Serves 4
Preparation time: 20 mins + 20 mins soaking time
Cooking time: 15 mins

Stir-fried Vegetarian Rice Vermicelli

Rice vermicelli is a popular alternative to wheat noodles in vegetarian cooking, and is an excellent choice for those who do not tolerate wheat products well.

6 large dried *shiitake* mushrooms, soaked in hot water 20 minutes
1 teaspoon soy sauce
1 teaspoon salt
6$^1/_2$ oz (200 g) dried rice vermicelli
1 tablespoon sesame oil
2 tablespoons vegetable oil
$^1/_2$ in (1 cm) fresh ginger, julienned
2 cloves garlic, minced
1 teaspoon sugar
$^1/_2$ teaspoon salt
2 cups (200 g) cabbage, finely shredded
1 small carrot, julienned
1 bunch garlic chives, snipped into 2-in (5-cm) lengths
1 tablespoon vegetarian mushroom oyster sauce
1 cup fresh bean sprouts, washed and trimmed
1 teaspoon freshly ground black pepper
1 red chili, sliced, for garnish
2 limes, cut in wedges

1 After soaking mushrooms, remove stems and slice mushrooms, reserving soaking liquid. Set mushrooms aside.

2 Bring a pot of water with the salt to a full boil, and add the rice vermicelli. Cook for exactly 3 minutes, and drain. Place noodles in a mixing bowl and drizzle with sesame oil; toss to coat thoroughly and set aside.

3 Heat oil in a wok until smoking, and add the ginger, garlic, and *shiitake* mushrooms and stir-fry 1 to 2 minutes. Add the soy sauce, sugar, and salt, and stir-fry.

4 Add the cabbage and carrot and stir-fry for 2 to 3 minutes; stir in 3 tablespoons of the reserved *shiitake* water and cook for 2 to 3 minutes more.

5 Add the garlic chives and vegetarian mushroom oyster sauce and stir-fry for 2 minutes, and add the bean sprouts and stir-fry 1 minute more.

6 Add the black pepper, stir to distribute evenly, and place vegetables on the rice vermicelli. Toss to combine, garnish with the sliced chili, and serve with slices of lime.

Serves 4
Preparation time: **15 mins + 20 mins soaking time**
Cooking time: **30 mins**

Stir-fried Vegetarian Brown Rice

Many of the ingredients, such as *shiitake* and seaweed, may have possible medicinal properties. You may omit *konbu* and use a vegetable broth instead. You may also try other combinations of vegetables, such as corn, turnips, and other mushrooms.

1 cup (220 g) raw brown rice

Two 6-in (15-cm) strips dried *konbu*, soaked in $2^1/_2$ cups (625 ml) cool water for 20 minutes

2 tablespoons oil

1 cup (200 g) onions, thinly sliced

4 cloves garlic, minced

1 carrot, halved lengthwise, and sliced thinly

1 green bell pepper, seeded and diced

6 large dried *shiitake* mushrooms, soaked in hot water and diced

$^1/_2$ cup (80 g) fresh or frozen green peas

Fresh coriander leaves (cilantro) for garnish

Seasonings

$^1/_2$ teaspoon salt

1 teaspoon sugar

2 teaspoon soy sauce

1 teaspoon freshly ground black pepper

1 Slice *konbu* into $^1/_2$-in ($2^1/_2$-cm) strips and return to soaking liquid. Place *konbu* and water in a sauce-pan and bring to a boil. Reduce heat to low and cook for about 20 minutes, until liquid is reduced.

2 Place drained rice, *konbu* and *konbu* broth in a saucepan, bring to a boil over medium heat, and cook until the rice is tender, about 25 minutes. Cool rice and remove *konbu*.

3 Heat 2 tablespoons oil in wok or large skillet until hot, and add onion and garlic. Stir-fry for 1 minute. Add the carrots, green pepper, *shiitake*, peas, and seasonings. Continue to stir-fry for 2 to 3 minutes, then add the cooked rice and *konbu*. Mix well and cook until rice is heated through, about 5 minutes. Adjust seasonings.

4 Remove from the heat, and transfer rice and vegetables to a serving bowl.

Serves 4
Preparation time: **20 mins + overnight soaking**
Cooking time: **1 hour**

Spicy Stuffed Potatoes in Tomato Curry

4 large potatoes
2 tablespoons oil
1 cup (200 g) onions, diced
1 in (2$^1/_2$ cm) fresh ginger
2 cloves garlic
3 tomatoes, sliced
1 medium onion, peeled and thinly sliced
$^1/_2$ teaspoon ground cumin
1 teaspoon ground turmeric
1 teaspoon *garam masala*
$^1/_2$ teaspoon cayenne pepper
3 tablespoons yogurt
3 tablespoons coconut milk or milk
1 cup (250 ml) water
1$^1/_4$ teaspoons salt
Fresh coriander leaves (cilantro) to garnish, chopped

Stuffing
$^1/_3$ cup (30 g) almonds, blanched and chopped
$^1/_3$ cup (30 g) cashew nuts, chopped
$^1/_3$ cup (30 g) pistachio nuts, chopped
$^2/_3$ cup (80 g) raisins, chopped
3 tablespoons sour cream or yogurt
1 teaspoon cayenne pepper
Pinch of salt

1 Boil or bake the potatoes until partially cooked, about 10 minutes, then halve them lengthwise. Scoop out some of the insides with a spoon, leaving about a $^1/_4$-in ($^1/_2$-cm) thick wall of potato.
2 Mix the scooped potato flesh with all the stuffing ingredients. Place 1 tablespoon of the stuffing back into each potato half. Tie two halves of the stuffed potatoes with a kitchen string and set aside.
3 Heat oil and fry the 1 cup of sliced onions until golden brown. Set aside.
4 Grind the fried onions, ginger, garlic, and tomatoes to form a paste.
5 Heat oil and sauté the onions until golden brown. Add the blended ingredients and the spices — cumin, turmeric, masala, and cayenne pepper. Reduce to low heat until the oil separates.
6 Add the yogurt, milk, water, and salt. Bring to a boil and cook for 3 minutes. Add the potatoes and continue to cook for another 5 minutes.
7 Cover and cook until the gravy becomes thick and coats the stuffed potatoes. Garnish with coriander leaves and serve.

Serves 4
Preparation time: **15 mins**
Cooking time: **45 mins**

Curried Potatoes and Chickpeas

1 cup (200 g) dried chickpeas, (*channa dal*) soaked in water for 5 hours; or
1 can chickpeas, rinsed
1 to 2 tablespoons oil
1 cup (170 g) potatoes, washed and cubed
2 tablespoons ghee or oil plus extra oil for frying
1 teaspoon cumin seeds
2 bay leaves
1 cup (200 g) onions, thinly sliced
2 large ripe tomatoes, thinly sliced
2 tablespoons ground coriander
1 tablespoon ground cumin
2 tablespoons cayenne pepper
1 teaspoon ground turmeric
2 teaspoons *garam masala*
1^1/$_2$ teaspoons salt
1^1/$_2$ cups water
1^1/$_2$ tablespoons lime or lemon juice
1 tablespoon fresh ginger, julienned
2 tablespoons fresh coriander leaves (cilantro), chopped

1 Place soaked chickpeas in a pan and add water to cover, bring to the boil, and cook until tender, about 30 minutes. Drain and set aside.
2 Heat oil in a skillet. Fry the cubed potatoes until golden brown. Remove from the heat and set aside.
3 Heat the ghee or oil in the wok over medium heat. Add the cumin seeds and bay leaves and fry until aromatic. Add the onion slices and sauté over low heat until the onion turns golden brown, about 5 minutes.
4 Add the tomatoes, coriander, cumin, chili, and turmeric powders, *garam masala* and salt, reduce the heat to low and cook until the oil separates.
5 Add the chickpeas, fried potatoes, and the water. Bring to a boil and cook for 5 minutes. Remove from the heat.
6 Stir in the lime juice, ginger, and coriander leaves before serving.

To avoid frying, add the cubed potatoes to the pan of boiling chickpeas after 15 minutes (Step 1).

Serves 4–6
Preparation time: 20 mins + 5 hours soaking time
Cooking time: 40 mins

Curried Yellow Lentils with Spinach

1 cup (200 g) yellow lentils (*tur dal*), washed and drained
5 cups (1 1/4 liters) water
1/2 teaspoon ground turmeric
2 green chilies, seeded and slit lengthwise
4 cloves garlic
1 lb (500 g) spinach leaves, washed and chopped
1 teaspoon ground cumin
1/2 teaspoon cayenne pepper
1 1/2 teaspoons salt
2 tablespoons ghee, butter or oil
1 teaspoon mustard seeds
1/2 teaspoon cumin seeds
1/2 teaspoon fennel seeds
2 dried chilies, cut into 1-in (3-cm) pieces
1/2 cup (100 g) onions, thinly sliced

1 Place lentils, water, turmeric, green chilies, and garlic cloves into a pan. Bring to the boil and cook over medium heat until the lentils soften, about 15 minutes.
2 Add the chopped spinach, cumin, chili, and salt. Cover and cook until the spinach has wilted.
3 In a separate pan, heat ghee or oil over medium heat and fry the mustard, cumin, fennel seeds, and the chilies until light brown.
4 Add the onions and stir-fry until golden brown.
5 Transfer the fried spices and onions to the first pan. Cook for a further 2 minutes, then switch off the heat.

Serves 4–6
Preparation time: **15 mins**
Cooking time: **30 mins**

Bell Pepper Masala

2 tablespoons oil
1 teaspoon fennel seeds
$1/2$ teaspoon cumin seeds
4 cardamom pods
1 cup (200 g) onions,
  thinly sliced
4 large ripe tomatoes,
  thinly sliced
2 tablespoons ginger,
  grated
1 tablespoon garlic,
  crushed
1 tablespoon sesame
  seeds, roasted and
  pounded
2 teaspoons cayenne
  pepper
2 teaspoons ground
  coriander seeds
2 teaspoons ground
  turmeric
1 teaspoon *garam
  masala*
$1^1/4$ teaspoons salt
1 teaspoon sugar
1 teaspoon lime juice or
  vinegar
$1/4$ cup water
12 oz (300 g) green bell
  peppers, seeded and
  sliced lengthwise

1 Heat oil in a large skillet over medium heat and fry the fennel, cumin seeds, and cardamoms until fragrant.
2 Add the onion slices and sauté until golden brown.
3 Add the tomatoes, ginger, garlic, sesame seeds, chili, coriander, turmeric, and *garam masala*. Reduce the heat to low and cook for 10 minutes or until the oil separates.
4 Add the remaining ingredients. Mix well, cover and cook until the bell peppers are soft, about 5 minutes. Serve hot.

Serves 4–6
Preparation time: 25 mins
Cooking time: 20 mins

Indian-style Vegetables in Coconut Milk

$^1/_2$ cup (80 g) cashew
  nuts
$^3/_4$ cup (180 ml)
  coconut milk or milk
2 tablespoons ghee or
  butter or oil
2 in (5 cm) cinnamon
  stick
6 cardamom pods
6 cloves
1 teaspoon fennel seeds,
  coarsely ground
1 cup (200 g) onions,
  thinly sliced
2 sprigs curry leaves
4 tablespoons curry
  powder
2 tablespoons fresh
  ginger, grated
2 tablespoons garlic,
  minced
5 cups (1$^1/_4$ liter) water
1 cup (100 g) sliced
  fresh mushrooms
1$^1/_2$ cups (300 g)
  potatoes, peeled
  and diced
1 cup (200 g) carrots,
  diced
1 cup (200 g) tomatoes,
  diced
1 cup (120 g) fresh or
  frozen peas
1$^1/_2$ teaspoons salt
2 tablespoons fresh
  coriander leaves
  (cilantro), chopped
1 tablespoon lime or
  lemon juice

1 In a blender, blend cashew nuts and coconut milk until very smooth. Set aside.

2 Heat ghee in a wok over medium heat and fry the cinnamon, cardamoms, cloves and fennel seeds until aromatic. Add the onions and curry leaves and sauté for 2 minutes until golden brown.

3 Mix the curry powder with the ginger and garlic, add to the pan, reduce the heat to low, and cook until the oil separates, about 2 minutes.

4 Add the water, mushrooms, diced vegetables, peas, and salt. Cover and cook over medium heat until the vegetables are cooked, about 15 minutes. Two minutes before the end of cooking add the cashew nut mixture.

5 Remove from the heat and stir in the coriander leaves and lime juice.

Serves 4–6
Preparation time: **25 mins**
Cooking time: **25 mins**

Curried Peas and Mushrooms with Tomatoes and Cashews

2 tablespoons ghee or oil
2 in (5 cm) cinnamon
  stick, broken in half
5 cloves
5 cardamom pods
$1/2$ cup (100 g) onions,
  finely sliced
$1^1/2$ tablespoons fresh
  ginger, grated
$1^1/2$ tablespoons garlic,
  crushed
3 medium tomatoes,
  chopped
2 tablespoons ground
  coriander
1 tablespoon cayenne
  pepper
1 teaspoon ground
  turmeric
2 teaspoons *garam
  masala*
$1^1/2$ teaspoons salt
$1^1/2$ cups (375 ml) water
2 cups (200 g) button
  mushrooms, sliced
$1^1/2$ cups (230 g) fresh
  or frozen peas
$1/2$ cup (80 g) cashew
  nuts blended with
  $1/2$ cup (125 ml)
  water until smooth
$1^1/2$ tablespoons tomato
  purée
2 tablespoons fresh
  coriander leaves
  (cilantro), chopped

1 Heat oil in skillet over medium heat and fry the cinnamon sticks, cloves, and cardamoms until aromatic. Add the sliced onion and sauté until golden brown.

2 Add the ginger-garlic paste and sauté for 1 minute. Add the tomatoes, and coriander, chili, turmeric and *garam masala* powders. Cook over low heat until the oil separates, about 5 minutes.

3 Add salt and water and bring to the boil. Add the mushrooms, green peas, cashew nut mixture, and tomato purée.

4 Cover and cook for 5 minutes, stirring occasionally. Remove from heat and sprinkle with chopped coriander leaves before serving.

Serves 4–6
Preparation time: **25 mins**
Cooking time: **15 mins**

Malaysian Sour and Sweet Pineapple Curry

3 tablespoons oil
5 shallots, sliced
2 cloves garlic, minced
1$^{1}/_{4}$ in (3 cm) stick
  cinnamon
4 cloves
1 whole star anise
3 cardamom pods, slit
  and bruised
1 small pineapple, (2 lbs
  or 1 kg), peeled and
  cut in bite-sized pieces
$^{2}/_{3}$ to 1 cup (80 to 120 g)
  palm sugar, crushed,
  or more to taste
1 to 2 large red chilies,
  left whole
1 cup coconut milk
1 teaspoon salt
1 green chili, halved
  lengthwise, seeds
  removed

Spice Paste
1 tablespoon fresh
  coriander seeds
$^{1}/_{2}$ teaspoon cumin
$^{1}/_{2}$ teaspoon fennel
5 shallots, chopped
2 cloves garlic, minced
1 large red chili, sliced
1 teaspoon ground
  turmeric
$^{1}/_{2}$ teaspoon salt

1 To prepare the spice paste, cook the coriander, cumin, and fennel in a dry skillet over low heat until fragrant, about 2 minutes. Transfer to a spice grinder and grind to a powder.

2 In a blender, grind the shallots, garlic, chilies, turmeric, and salt to form a smooth paste, adding a little oil if necessary to keep the mixture turning. Add the powered spice to the paste, and set aside.

3 Heat the oil in a saucepan, add shallots and garlic, and stir-fry over medium heat until golden. Add the spice paste, cinnamon, cloves, star anise, and cardamom and stir-fry until fragrant, 3 to 4 minutes. Add the pineapple, sugar and red chilies, and cook over low to medium heat, stirring frequently, 5 minutes.

4 Add the coconut milk, bring to the boil, reduce heat to low, and cook, uncovered, 5 minutes. Add the green chilies and continue cooking until the pineapple is soft, 2 to 3 minutes. Transfer to a serving dish.

Serves 4 to 6
Preparation time: **20–25 mins**
Cooking time: **20 mins**

Eggplant and Lentil Curry

$^1/_2$ cup (100 g) yellow mung beans (*mung dal*), washed and drained

$^1/_2$ teaspoon ground turmeric

1 teaspoon ghee or oil

2 cups (500 ml) water

12 oz (300 g) eggplant, cubed

1 teaspoon ground cumin

2 teaspoons cayenne pepper

$^1/_4$ cup (50 g) tamarind juice (see page 7)

1$^1/_4$ teaspoons salt

2 tablespoons oil

1 teaspoon black lentils (*urad dal*)

$^1/_2$ teaspoon mustard seeds

1 teaspoon cumin seeds

$^1/_2$ teaspoon fennel seeds, coarsely ground

$^1/_2$ cup (100 g) onions, thinly sliced

2 sprigs curry leaves

2 tablespoons fresh coriander leaves (cilantro), finely chopped

1 Place yellow mung beans, turmeric, ghee and water in a pan, bring to a boil, and cook over medium heat, about 10 minutes.

2 Add the eggplant, cumin and cayenne pepper, tamarind juice and salt. Cook until the eggplant is tender, about 8 minutes.

3 In a separate pan, heat the oil over medium heat and fry the black grams until golden brown about 4 minutes. Add the mustard and cumin seeds, and fennel. Fry until aromatic, about 2 minutes.

4 Add the onion and curry leaves and sauté until the onions become golden brown.

5 Transfer to the eggplant curry. Add the chopped coriander leaves and cook for 2 minutes more. Remove from the heat and serve.

Serves 4–6
Preparation time: **15 mins**
Cooking time: **25 mins**

Yellow Lentil 'Meatball' Curry

1¹/₄ cups (300 g) yellow lentils (*tur dal*), soaked for 3 hours

3 tablespoons split chickpeas *(channa dal)*, soaked for 3 hours

2 green chilies, seeded and cut into ¹/₂-in (1-cm) lengths

¹/₂ teaspoon ground turmeric

¹/₂ teaspoon salt

1 cup (100 g) carrot, finely grated

2 dried chilies, soaked

³/₄ teaspoon fenugreek

¹/₂ cup (80 g) tamarind juice (see page 7)

2 tablespoons oil

1 teaspoon cumin seeds

¹/₂ teaspoon mustard seeds

2 sprigs curry leaves

1 Drain the lentils and chickpeas and put them in a food processor or blender. Add the green chilies, turmeric and salt, and process. Stir in the grated carrot, and mix well.

2 Shape the mixture into small balls and place on a lightly oiled steamer tray. Steam for 10 minutes. Remove from the steamer and set aside.

3 In a food processor or blender, grind the dried chilies and fenugreek with the tamarind juice and set aside.

4 In a saucepan, heat the oil over medium heat and fry the cumin and mustard seeds and the curry leaves until aromatic. Add the chili-tamarind mixture, bring to a boil, and cook for about 10 minutes. Add the steamed balls. Return to the boil and cook for 5 minutes more.

Serves 4
Preparation time: **30 mins + 3 hours soaking**
Cooking time: **25 mins**

Curried Pumpkin

2 tablespoons oil
$^1/_2$ teaspoon mustard
seeds
1 teaspoon fennel seeds
$^1/_4$ teaspoon fenugreek
1 dried chili, cut into
1$^1/_4$ in (3 cm) long
pieces
1 cup (200 g) onions,
finely sliced
1 green chili, seeded
and cubed
1 lb (450 g) pumpkin,
seeded, skinned, and
cubed
1 cup (250 ml) water
1 teaspoon ground
turmeric
1 teaspoon cayenne
pepper
1 teaspoon ground cumin
1$^1/_2$ teaspoons salt
$^1/_4$ cup (50 g) tamarind
juice (see page 7)
$^1/_4$ cup (50 g) sugar

1 Heat oil in a large skillet and fry the mustard and
fennel seeds, fenugreek, and dried chilies until the
chilies turn brown.
2 Add the onion and green chilies and sauté for 2
minutes or until the onion turns golden brown.
3 Add the pumpkin, water, turmeric, chili and cumin
powders, and salt. Cover and cook over medium heat
until the pumpkin pieces are almost tender, about
15 minutes.
4 Add the tamarind juice and sugar and cook
until the liquid is absorbed and the pumpkin is soft.
Serve hot.

Serves 4–6
Preparation time: 15 mins
Cooking time: 25 mins

Chinese Vegetarian Sandwich with Sesame Spread

This modern adaptation of a sort of "Chinese sandwich" calls for a high-quality whole-grain bread, thinly sliced and toasted.

3 thin slices of whole-grain bread, toasted
1 tomato, thinly sliced
12 to 15 celery leaves, coarsely chopped
2 to 3 leaves iceberg lettuce
1 small onion, thinly sliced

Spread
$1/4$ cup (35 g) raw sunflower seeds, presoaked at least 3 hours in cool water and drained
2 tablespoons sesame paste or tahini, blended with 3 teaspoons water
$1/2$ tablespoon sesame oil
$1/4$ teaspoon salt
$1/2$ teaspoon sugar
1 teaspoon soy sauce
1 teaspoon freshly ground black pepper
Garlic to taste, roasted (optional)

1 To prepare the spread, place all the ingredients in a blender, and blend until smooth. Adjust seasonings, if necessary.
2 To assemble the sandwich, place a slice of toast on a plate and cover with one-quarter of the spread. Arrange half the tomato slices, chopped celery leaves, lettuce and onion slices on top of the spread. Top with a second slice of toast spread-side down, then cover the top of that slice with spread and arrange remaining vegetables on it. Complete the sandwich with the third slice of toast placed spread-side down.
3 Cut in half with sharp knife, or serve whole.

Serves 1
Preparation time: 10 mins
Assembling time: 5 mins

Split Chickpea Curry with Crispy Indian Pancake (pancake recipe on following page)

This delicious chickpea curry is just one of the many vegetable or meat curries that make an excellent accompaniment to *roti canai*.

$^1/_2$ cup (110 g) split chickpeas (*channa dal*), washed
$3^1/_2$ cups (875 ml) water
$^1/_4$ teaspoon ground turmeric
1 medium onion, cubed
1 small carrot, sliced
1 small eggplant, cubed
1 medium tomato, cut into wedges
1 green chili, cut into $^3/_4$-in (2-cm) lengths
Scant $^1/_2$ cup (100 ml) coconut milk or regular milk
Salt to taste
$^1/_2$ cup (125 ml) tamarind juice (page 6)
3 tablespoons oil
$^1/_2$ teaspoon black mustard seeds
$^1/_2$ teaspoon cumin seeds
1 sprig curry leaves
1 dried red chili, cut into $^3/_4$-in (2-cm) lengths
3 shallots, thinly sliced
3 cloves garlic, thinly sliced

1 Remove any grit from peas and put in a saucepan with water and turmeric. Bring to the boil and reduce heat to low, cook for 20 minutes.

2 Add onion, carrot, eggplant, and tomato. Cook for another 20 minutes, or until vegetables are tender. Add the green chilies during the last 5 minutes of cooking.

3 Add the coconut milk, salt, and tamarind juice. Cook for 5 minutes and remove pan from heat.

4 Meanwhile, heat oil in a skillet over medium heat and fry mustard and cumin seeds, for 30 seconds or until they pop. Add curry leaves, dried chilies, shallots, and garlic. Fry until shallots and garlic turn golden brown. Spoon into the pea mixture, stir well, cover pan, and remove from the heat.

Serves 4
Preparation time: 30 mins
Cooking time: 50 mins

Crispy Indian Pancake (Roti Canai)

Roti canai is a delicious crispy pancake and a favorite Malaysian dish, enjoyed and eaten throughout the day. This is an unconventional way to make *roti canai*, but it is an easier method for the home cook to follow than attempting to duplicate the skilled maneuvers of a *roti canai* cook.

Dough 1
3 cups (360 g) all-purpose flour
1 1/2 teaspoons salt
1 tablespoon sugar
2 oz (30 g) softened butter or vegetable oil
1 egg, beaten
1/2 cup (125 ml) regular milk
About 5 tablespoons water

Dough 2
1 1/2 cups (180 g) all-purpose flour
1/2 cup (130 g) softened butter or vegetable oil

1/2 tablespoon oil

Makes 16 pancakes
Preparation time: 30 mins
Standing time: 1–2 hours
Cooking time: 20 mins

1 To make Dough 1, combine flour, salt, and sugar in a mixing bowl. Add in the softened butter. Beat egg and milk together in a measuring cup and add enough water to make 1 cup liquid.

2 Using fingertips, mix the softened butter well. Pour 3/4 cup (180 ml) of the egg-milk mixture into the dry ingredients. Mix by hand to make a fairly soft, pliable dough. If dough seems dry, add remaining liquid a drop at a time. Once dough starts to bind, stop adding liquid.

3 Knead well on a lightly floured surface for 10 to 15 minutes, until the dough is smooth and elastic. Form into a thick "sausage" and divide into 8 equal pieces.

4 To make Dough 2, combine flour and butter in a bowl and mix with a fork until the mixture forms a soft, smooth dough. Divide into 8 pieces and roll each into a ball. Cover with a clean cloth and set aside.

5 To make the pancake, flatten one Dough 1 ball into a disk about 3 in (7 cm) in diameter. Place one Dough 2 ball on top and wrap the flat disk up and around the ball.

6 On a lightly floured surface, use a rolling pin to roll out the ball into a rectangle 5 x 6 $\frac{1}{2}$ in (13 x 16 cm). Starting from the longer side, roll the dough up tightly like a long, thin jellyroll.

7 Flatten the "jellyroll" into a thin sheet. Now roll it up from the short end to make a short, fat roll. Cut the roll into 2 equal halves.

8 Sit the dough on its side, then roll each piece out thinly with a rolling pin. You will get a thin circle of dough lightly marked with concentric circles which will fry up into a light, flaky disk.

9 Heat $\frac{1}{2}$ tablespoon oil on a griddle and cook *roti canai* on medium heat for 2 to 3 minutes on each side or until golden brown. When done, transfer onto a flat surface and, using cupped hands, press the *roti canai* from the outside towards the center to fluff the layers. Serve hot with lentil curry.

Healthy Chinese Rice and Soy Beans

You may use this extremely healthy and tasty rice-and-beans combo as the main staple dish to be combined with other vegetable dishes.

$1/2$ cup (100 g) dried
  soy beans
3 cups (750 ml) water
$1/2$ teaspoon salt
1 cup (220 g) brown rice,
  washed and soaked in
  2 cups (500 ml) water

Garnishes
1 carrot, diced and
  blanched
1 cup red and green bell
  pepper, finely chopped
1 bunch fresh coriander
  leaves (cilantro), finely
  chopped
2 scallions, finely
  chopped
Freshly ground black
  pepper, chili flakes and
  salt to taste

1 Clean and rinse soy beans well. Drain and place in a saucepan with water to cover by at least 1 in ($2^1/_2$ cm). Soak overnight.

2 The next day, drain water from soy beans and add 3 cups fresh water. Bring to the boil over medium heat, cover, and reduce heat to low. Cook until the beans absorb all the water, about $1^1/_2$ hours. Check the beans occasionally to make sure they don't scorch. When soft, transfer them to a bowl and set aside to cool.

3 Add salt to the soaked rice and bring to a full boil. Cover, reduce heat to very low, and cook for about 30 minutes, or until the rice starts to crackle. Do not remove lid while cooking. Remove from the heat and set aside, still covered, for 15 minutes. Transfer to a bowl and set aside to cool, turning the rice once or twice with a spoon to cool and dry evenly.

4 When rice and beans have cooled to warm, carefully fold them together in a large serving bowl. Stir in all or any of the garnishes and serve.

Serves 4
Preparation time: **overnight soaking**
Cooking time: **50 mins**

Indian Tomato Cashew Pilau Rice

2 tablespoons ghee or oil
Two 1-in (2$^1/_2$-cm)
  sticks cinnamon,
  broken in half
5 cloves
5 cardamom pods
2 cups (200 g) onions,
  thinly sliced
3 green chilies, seeded
  and slit lengthwise
2 tablespoons ginger,
  grated
2 tablespoons garlic,
  crushed
3 tablespoons fresh
  coriander leaves
  (cilantro), chopped
3 tablespoons mint
  leaves, chopped
2$^1/_2$ cups (500 g) basmati
  rice, washed and
  drained
2 cups (300 g) tomatoes,
  blanched and chopped
1 cup (250 ml) thick
  coconut milk
1 teaspoon ground
  turmeric
1$^1/_2$ teaspoons salt
2$^1/_2$ cups (625 ml) water
$^1/_4$ cup (40 g) raisins
$^1/_2$ cup (80 g) cashew
  nuts, fried or roasted

1 Heat the ghee or oil in a skillet over medium heat. Fry the whole spices — cinnamon, cloves, and cardamom — and the onions, green chilies, ginger and garlic pastes until the onions are golden brown, or about 10 minutes.

2 Add the coriander and mint leaves, then stir in the rice and mix well.

3 Add the remaining ingredients except for the raisins and cashew nuts and mix thoroughly.

4 Cover with a tight-fitting lid, reduce the heat to low, and cook for 15 to 20 minutes. Alternatively, transfer the mixture to an electric rice cooker and cook according to the manufacturer's instructions.

5 Stir occasionally until the rice is cooked and all the moisture has been absorbed.

6 Fluff the rice up and mix in the raisins and cashew nuts just before serving. Serve hot.

Basmati rice *is an Indian long-grain rice charactized by its thinness and fragrance. The grains stay whole and separate when cooked with oil and spices. Substitute with 1 cup wild rice mixed with 1$^1/_2$ cups long-grain white rice*

Serves 4–6
Preparation time: **15 mins**
Cooking time: **25 mins**

Malaysian Coastal Traders' Vegetarian Rice

1 cup (100 g) white glutinous rice
1 cup (100 g) red or brown long-grain or wild rice
1 cup (250 ml) coconut milk
$^3/_4$ cup (180 ml) water
$1^1/_2$ teaspoons salt
6 to 8 pandanus leaves, or several drops vanilla extract
$^1/_4$ teaspoon fenugreek seeds
One $^3/_4$-in ($1^1/_2$-cm) piece fresh ginger, minced
3 shallots, thinly sliced

1 Mix the glutinous and long-grain rice then place in a rice cooker with the coconut milk, water, salt and pandanus leaves, if using.
2 Cook the rice, and when most of the liquid has been absorbed, stir in the fenugreek seeds, ginger and shallots. Discard the pandanus leaves, or add the vanilla extract, if using. Cover again and let rice cook for another 15–20 minutes.
3 Fluff the rice with a fork to separate the grains and serve hot.

This recipe traditionally uses red glutinous rice and is delicious served with spicy salads and curries.

Serves 4
Preparation time: **15 mins**
Cooking time: **40 mins**

Sweet Green Lentil Soup

If you prefer the soup chilled, let it cool after cooking, then put it in the refrigerator for a few hours prior to serving. Large quantities may be prepared in advance and kept for 4 to 5 days in the refrigerator; this makes a very refreshing and healthy summer snack. You may also flavor the soup by adding a cinnamon stick or some grated nutmeg to the water.

1/2 cup (100 g) green
  lentils, picked clean
  and washed thoroughly
3 pandanus leaves, tied
  in a knot, or 1 teaspoon
  vanilla extract
4 cups (1 liter) water
5 tablespoons sugar

1 Soak lentils overnight and drain. Place the lentils and pandanus leaves in a pan with 4 cups water and bring to a boil. Reduce heat to medium–low and stir in sugar. Cook until beans are soft, about 45 minutes.
2 Adjust the sweetness, if necessary. Discard leaves and serve in individual bowls.

Makes 4 small bowls
Preparation time: **overnight soaking**
Cooking time: **10 mins**

Chinese Sweet Red Date Soup with Lotus Seeds

This is both a popular Chinese dessert soup and a traditional Chinese herbal remedy for high blood pressure, arterioscelorsis, insomnia and immune defiency. All the ingredients are important items in the Chinese herbal pharmocopeia, and together they provide a potent tonic boost to the human energy system. According to Chinese lore, this soup should be served hot; eating it cold counteracts the medicinal benefits.

3 whole florets white (wood ear) fungus, soaked in cool water for 1 hour
30 dried white lotus seeds, soaked in cool water overnight
12 Chinese red dates or jujubes, washed and pits removed
6 cups (1 1/2 liters) water
1/2 cup (75 g) rock crystal sugar

Serves 4
Preparation time:
 overnight soaking
Cooking time: 1 1/2 hours

1 Drain the white fungus, trim, and discard the tough bases. Shred and set aside.
2 Drain the lotus seeds and place in a large pot with the red dates, white fungus and water.
3 Bring to a boil, and add rock sugar. Cover, reduce heat to low, and cook for 1 hour.
4 Adjust for sweetness, if necessary. Transfer the soup to a tureen or ladle into individual serving bowls. Serve hot.

Red dates are also known as Chinese jujube, or hong zao in Mandarin. Chinese red dates are the size of a round olive and, although sour when green, are sweet when matured and dried. Red dates are often eaten during Chinese New Year

Sweet Pumpkin and Lotus Seed Soup

For variation, you may add a cinnamon stick, split vanilla bean, or other aromatic spices to the soup while cooking. If you like the taste, try using $^2/_3$ cup (80 ml) of maple syrup for a sweetener in place of the rock sugar, or using $^1/_4$ cup (37 g) rock sugar and $^1/_3$ cup (40 ml) maple syrup.

$^1/_2$ lb (225 g) pumpkin, peeled, seeded and cubed (about 3 cups)
8 cups (2 liters) water
1 whole floret white fungus, soaked in cool water for 1 hour
20 dried white lotus seeds, soaked overnight in cool water and drained
$^1/_2$ cup (75 g) rock crystal sugar
1 tablespoon cornstarch or water chestnut flour stirred in 1 tablespoon water

1 Put pumpkin and water in a large pot, bring to a boil, and reduce heat to medium.

2 Drain the white fungus and trim and discard tough stems. Roughly shred and add fungus, lotus seeds, and rock sugar to pot. Cover and return to boil, reduce heat to low, and cook for 50 minutes.

3 Stir the cornstarch mixture, and add to the soup. Stir for 1 minute, cover, and cook for another 10 minutes. Remove from heat and serve.

Serves 4
Preparation time: **10 mins + overnight soaking**
Cooking time: **1$^1/_2$ hours**

Shaved Ice with Red Beans

You really need an ice-shaving machine to make this dessert properly, but if you do not have one, you can put ice cubes in a blender, although this will make it more like a drink than the dessert that it is. Although not widely available, cooked, sweetened red kidney beans can be bought in tins. If you are unable to obtain them, you can make them from scratch.

1 cup (200 g) red kidney or azuki beans
Sugar to taste
1 cup (200 g) seaweed jelly, finely chopped
1 cup (300 g) creamed corn
1 cup (250 ml) evaporated milk
2/3 cup (150 ml) fruit-flavored or rose syrup
2/3 cup (150 ml) brown sugar, palm sugar, or maple syrup
Freshly shaved ice or crushed ice cubes

Serves 4
Preparation time: **10 mins**
Assembling time: **10 mins**

1 Rinse beans and soak until plump (soak kidney beans overnight, adzuki beans for 1 to 2 hours). Rinse beans and cover with 4 cups (1 liter) fresh water. Bring beans and water to boil in a large pan and cook until beans are tender. (They should be soft but still hold their shape, about 40 minutes for the small adzuki beans and 1 1/2 hours for the larger kidney beans). Sweeten to taste. Set aside to cool.

2 To serve, place a generous spoonful of beans, seaweed jelly, and corn in a deep serving bowl. Top with a mound of shaved ice and drizzle in a spoonful each of fruit and brown sugar syrups. Pour on 1 to 2 tablespoons of evaporated milk and serve immediately.

Palm sugar syrup can be made by chopping up chunks of the palm sugar and adding a little water, cooking over low heat until it caramelizes.

Coconut Custard in Pumpkin

1 small pumpkin, 3 to 4 lb ($1^1/_2$ to 2 kg), thoroughly
  washed
4 large eggs
$1^1/_3$ cups (200 g) palm sugar, finely shaved with a
  knife, or maple syrup
1 to 2 tablespoons sugar
5 pandanus leaves, scraped with a fork and tied
  together to form a whisk, or several drops
  vanilla extract
1 cup (250 ml) thick coconut milk
$^1/_2$ teaspoon ground cinnamon
$^1/_4$ teaspoon salt

1 Slice off the top part of the pumpkin and reserve to
use as a lid. Scoop out the seeds and fibers. Wash, drain,
and pat dry with paper towels. Replace the lid of the
pumpkin and steam over boiling water for 15 minutes.
2 Put eggs and both sugars in a bowl and stir with
the tied pandanus leaves until the eggs are well
mixed. Add vanilla extract (if using), coconut milk,
cinnamon, and salt, and stir to mix thoroughly.
3 Pour the coconut milk mixture into the pumpkin,
and cover with the lid. Place inside a steamer and
cook over medium heat until the custard has set,
35 to 40 minutes. Remove pumpkin and set aside to
cool. Cut into slices and serve at room temperature.

Serves 4 to 6
Preparation time: **20 mins**
Cooking time: **1 hour**

Sweet Potato and Taro in Coconut Milk

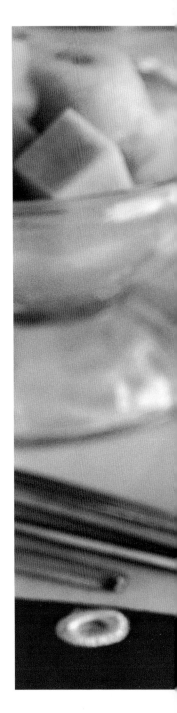

1 small taro, about 6¹/₂ oz (200 g), peeled and cubed
1 small sweet potato, about 6¹/₂ oz (200 g), peeled and cubed
1 pandanus leaf, tied into a knot or a few drops vanilla extract
3 cups (750 ml) water
1 cup (250 ml) coconut milk
About ¹/₂ cup (100 g) sugar or chopped palm sugar, or ¹/₂ cup (125 ml) maple syrup
Pinch salt
2 ripe bananas, peeled and cut diagonally into ¹/₂-in (1-cm) slices

1 Place taro, sweet potato and pandanus leaf in a medium saucepan with the water and bring to boil over medium-high heat. Reduce the heat to medium and cook until the taro and sweet potato are tender, 15 to 20 minutes.
2 Add coconut milk, sugar, and salt and return to the boil. Add the sliced bananas and cook for 3 minutes more. Serve warm or cold.

Serves 5 to 8
Preparation time: **20 mins**
Cooking time: **30 mins**

Tropical Mango Pudding

²/₃ cup (150 ml) water
  (at room temperature)
3 teaspoons powdered
  agar-agar
4 to 6 tablespoons
  superfine sugar
1 or 2 ripe mangoes,
  about 14 oz (450 g)
²/₃ cup (150 ml) whole
  milk
²/₃ cup (150 ml)
  evaporated milk

Makes six ¹/₂ cup jelly
  moulds
Preparation time: **10 mins**
Chilling time: **1 hour**

1 Pour water into a heatproof bowl. Set aside for 10 to 15 minutes until agar-agar absorbs the water and looks swollen and spongy. Dissolve the agar-agar by sitting the bowl in a larger bowl of hot water — stir until agar-agar is totally dissolved and there are no more lumps. Stir the sugar into the agar-agar.

2 Peel mangoes and cut the flesh away from the stone in two halves. Dice one-half of the mango and set aside. Cube the remaining half of the mango. Place mango cubes and whole milk in an electric blender or food processor and process.

3 Combine the agar-agar mixture, evaporated milk, puréed mango and diced mango. Stir well and pour into small glass bowls. Chill well until set before serving.

Sweet Corn Pudding

This corn pudding can be served turned out of its mould and surrounded by a spoonful of evaporated milk. Alternatively, you can also pour the hot pudding mixture into a glass dish or cake pan. After a thorough chilling, cut the pudding into squares and serve. The sliced pudding needs to be firmer to ensure easy cutting, so increase the quantity of green pea flour from $^1/_2$ cup (60 g) to $^2/_3$ cup (80 g).

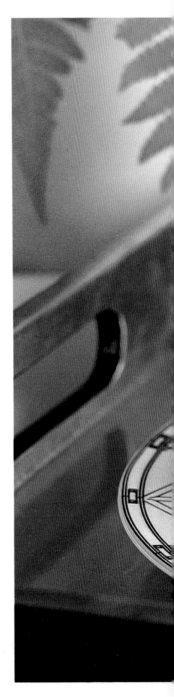

2$^1/_2$ cups (600 ml) coconut milk
$^1/_2$ cup (60 g) green pea flour
$^3/_4$ cup (180 g) sugar
2 pandanus leaves, tied into a knot, or 1 teaspoon vanilla extract
1 cup (300 g) canned creamed corn

1 Combine coconut milk, flour and sugar in a saucepan and stir until well mixed. Add pandanus leaf or vanilla extract (if using) and creamed corn.
2 Cook over medium-low heat, stirring continuously with a wooden spoon, until mixture simmers and becomes thick and smooth. Continue to cook about 4 minutes more. Remove from the heat and discard pandanus leaf.
3 Spoon mixture into small jelly moulds and let puddings cool at room temperature before chilling in the refrigerator.

Makes one 8 in (20 cm) ring mould
Preparation time: **10 mins**
Cooking time: **10 mins**

Complete Recipe List